The Flavors of

BON APPÉTIT

2003

Romaine Salad with Chives
and Blue Cheese (page 146)

The Flavors of
BON APPÉTIT
2003

from the Editors of Bon Appétit

Condé Nast Books

New York

For *Bon Appétit* Magazine

Barbara Fairchild, *Editor-in-Chief*
Tricia Callas O'Donnell, *Contributing Editor, Books*
Laurie Glenn Buckle, *Managing Editor*
Marcy MacDonald, *Editorial Operations Director*
Carri Marks Oosterbaan, *Editorial Production Director*
Lynne Hartung, *Editorial Production Manager*
Sybil Shimazu Neubauer, *Editorial Administrator*
Jordana Ruhland, *Editorial Associate*
Marcia Hartmann Lewis, *Editorial Support*
Susan Champlin, *Text*
Shayna Sobol, *Copy Editor*
Gaylen Ducker Grody, *Research*
Elizabeth A. Matlin, *Index*

For Condé Nast Books

Lisa Faith Phillips, *Vice President and General Manager*
Tom Downing, *Direct Marketing Director*
Deborah Williams, *Operations Director*
Lyn Barris, *Project Manager*
Fianna Reznik, *Direct Marketing Associate*
Eric Levy, *Inventory Assistant*
Eric Killer, *Project Assistant*

Design: Monica Elias and Ph.D

Front Jacket: Sour Cream Layer Cake with Pecan Brittle (page 198)
Facing Page: Top: Yellow Tomato Gazpacho with Cilantro Oil and Avocado (page 32)
　　　　　　　Middle: Short Ribs Provençale with Crème Fraiche Mashed Potatoes (page 44)
　　　　　　　Bottom: Berry Streusel Pie (page 170)

Published by Condé Nast Books, Random House Direct, Inc., New York, New York.
A wholly owned subsidiary of Random House, Inc.

Printed in the United States of America

Library of Congress Cataloging-in-Publication Data is available upon request.

10 9 8 7 6 5 4 3 2 1

FIRST EDITION

Condé Nast Web Address: bonappetit.com
Bon Appétit Books Web Address: bonappetitbooks.com

Contents

Introduction

Every flavor represents a moment in time.

A bite of Grilled Spareribs with Cherry Cola Glaze, for instance, is not just a luscious combination of tender pork marinated in a sweet, salty, tangy sauce (though it's certainly that)—it's also the sultry summer day you spent at your best friend's backyard barbecue, cold beer in hand, while the kids shrieked and squirted each other with the garden hose. The most delicious taste experiences are recipes for indelible memories.

That's a big part of what this book is all about. *The Flavors of Bon Appétit 2003*, the tenth volume in our annual series, is designed to help you recollect—and re-create—the best dishes of the year, and to create the special moments that go with them. (By the way, the recipe for those Grilled Spareribs is on page 67.)

Each issue of *Bon Appétit* casts a wide net, capturing the freshest flavors of the

Grilled Spareribs with Cherry Cola Glaze
(page 67)

day and showcasing them in recipes you want to try right now, this minute. Because we're at the forefront of the food world, we know what ingredients are most in favor with chefs—and which are the classic staples of any thoughtfully stocked pantry. We track food trends—or, more often, set them. We celebrate the best of each season: its produce, its parties, its aromas, its sensations.

By the end of the year, we have presented hundreds of unforgettable recipes that offer a kind of culinary montage of the seasons' evolution.

The cycle begins with the hearty comfort foods of winter, the ones that bring you indoors from the rain, snow, and cold: Hot Chocolate with Vanilla Whipped Cream (page 36), Caramelized Onion and Portobello Mushroom Soup with Goat Cheese Croutons (page 26), Braised Lamb Shanks with Ginger and Five-Spice (page 60).

Spring Vegetable Paella (page 104)

As the weather warms, fresh asparagus, strawberries, and baby greens move to center stage; the rich flavors of winter give way to the light, bright tastes of spring. It's time for Easter egg hunts, Passover seders, and dishes such as Spring Vegetable Paella (page 104), Baked Salmon Stuffed with Mascarpone Spinach (page 95), and Strawberry and White Chocolate Mousse Tart (page 178).

Then comes summer. The idea alone gives the spirit a lift, carrying with it the anticipation of outdoor celebrations—family reunions, weddings, graduations, and vacations. The food moves outdoors, too, where you sip refreshing lime-and-rum Mojitos (page 40) while the barbecue serves up the aromas of Herb-Crusted Flank Steak with Cherry Tomatoes and Olives (page 46) or Grilled Corn on the Cob with Maple-Chipotle Glaze (page 139). A cool and colorful dessert is just the ticket to round out a summertime meal: How about Baked Alaskas with Spiced Peaches and Raspberries (page 220)?

And then it's time to come inside again—to head back to school or work, and

Tamarind-Glazed Lamb Skewers with Dried Apricot Relish (page 21)

prepare for the festive holiday feasts of fall. The entertaining ratchets up a notch, and you may find yourself ready to experiment with more ambitious recipes for your dinner guests—an Indian appetizer of Tamarind-Glazed Lamb Skewers with Dried Apricot Relish (page 21), or an elegant Austrian entrée of Roast Duck with Lingonberry Sauce (page 86).

You might have noticed something else while reading through these intriguing recipe titles: There is a wonderful variety of ethnic influences here, bringing a wealth of flavors, textures, and traditions to your dinner table.

While "Traditional American" and "Regional Italian" always top the list of reader preferences in our annual March readers' survey (and there are plenty of those Regional Italian recipes in this book—including an entire chapter on Pasta & Pizza), American diners also have been opening the kitchen door to many other types of cuisine: Nuevo-Latino (hence those Mojitos); Indian (as with those Tamarind Lamb Skewers); Moroccan (try the Chicken Tagine with Chickpeas and Green Beans on page 83); and all kinds of Asian

Chicken Tagine with Chickpeas and Green Beans (page 83)

dishes (like the Steamed Mussels in Thai Curry Sauce on page 22), among many others.

Blueberry Pancakes (page 110)

Because you are a *Bon Appétit* fan, you have an enthusiastic, enterprising spirit when it comes to food. You like to try new recipes, experiment with new ingredients, and open yourself up to the possibilities contained within the world of flavors. And because this is *Bon Appétit*, you know that you can count on these recipes to be accessible, foolproof, and absolutely delicious.

When you create the dishes in this book—whether you're returning to those simply terrific Blueberry Pancakes (page 110) that highlighted a long and lazy Sunday morning last August, or launching a new culinary adventure with Curried Couscous with Roasted Vegetables, Peach Chutney, and Cilantro Yogurt (page 108)—we're sure that the experience will later evoke memories for you and your friends of the first time you said, "This? Oh, I got the recipe from *Bon Appétit*."

Smoked Salmon Rolls with
Crème Fraîche (page 12)

Starters

Appetizers

Soups

Beverages

Smoked Salmon Rolls with Crème Fraîche

12 4x2½-inch slices smoked salmon

¾ cup (about) crème fraîche or sour cream

¾ cup chopped fresh basil

12 large fresh basil leaves

Place 1 salmon slice on work surface. Spread 2 teaspoons crème fraîche over salmon. Sprinkle with 2 teaspoons chopped basil. Sprinkle with pepper. Starting at 1 short end, roll up salmon slice, enclosing filling. Spread 1 teaspoon crème fraîche over top of roll; sprinkle with 1 teaspoon chopped basil. Cut roll crosswise into 5 slices (keep sliced roll together). Repeat with remaining salmon, crème fraîche, and chopped basil. *(Can be made 6 hours ahead. Transfer salmon rolls to plate. Cover and refrigerate.)*

Arrange basil leaves on platter. Using small spatula, top each basil leaf with 1 sliced salmon roll, fanning slightly.

6 SERVINGS

Whole Wheat Pita Chips with Garbanzo Bean-Cumin Dip

2 whole wheat pita bread rounds

2 teaspoons ground cumin

1 15-ounce can garbanzo beans (chickpeas), drained, liquid reserved

2 tablespoons fresh lemon juice

1 tablespoon extra-virgin olive oil

1 small garlic clove, peeled

Preheat oven to 350°F. Cut each whole wheat pita bread round horizontally along folded edges, forming 4 rounds total. Stack pita rounds on work surface; cut stack into 8 wedges, forming 32 wedges total. Place pita wedges in single layer on baking sheet. Bake until wedges are crisp and golden, about 10 minutes. Cool completely.

Stir cumin in small dry skillet over medium-low heat until fragrant, about 30 seconds. Remove from heat. Combine garbanzo beans, 3 tablespoons reserved garbanzo bean liquid, lemon juice, oil, garlic, and cumin in processor. Puree until smooth, adding more garbanzo bean liquid by tablespoonfuls for desired consistency. Season to taste with salt and pepper. Transfer dip to bowl. *(Pita chips and dip can be prepared 4 days ahead. Store chips in resealable plastic bag at room temperature. Cover and refrigerate dip.)* Serve dip with pita chips.

4 SERVINGS

Brie and Chive Toasts with Arugula

20 ¾-inch-thick slices French-bread baguette

 1 cup chopped fresh chives

¾ pound Brie, rind removed

60 arugula leaves (about 2 cups packed)

Preheat oven to 400°F. Arrange bread on large baking sheet. Toast until golden, about 5 minutes. Cool toasts. Maintain oven temperature.

Sprinkle each toast with 1 teaspoon chives, then spread with 1 heaping tablespoon cheese. Top with 1 teaspoon chives and sprinkle with pepper. Bake until toasts are warm and cheese begins to melt, about 2 minutes. Transfer toasts to serving platter. Top each with 3 arugula leaves. Serve warm.

MAKES 20

Spicy Marinated Mozzarella with Oregano and Capers

12 ounces fresh water-packed mozzarella cheese, drained, cut into ¼-inch-thick slices

6 tablespoons extra-virgin olive oil
2 garlic cloves, minced
¼ teaspoon dried crushed red pepper
1 tablespoon minced fresh oregano
¼ teaspoon coarse salt
¼ teaspoon ground black pepper
2 tablespoons capers, chopped

Overlap cheese slices on medium platter.

Heat 2 tablespoons olive oil in small skillet over medium heat. Add minced garlic and crushed red pepper and stir just until garlic begins to color, about 2 minutes. Remove from heat; stir in oregano, salt, and pepper. Cool. Stir in capers and remaining 4 tablespoons olive oil. Spoon over cheese slices.

6 SERVINGS

Tomato-Dill Fritters

1½ pounds plum tomatoes, halved, seeded, chopped (about 4 cups)
1 cup chopped red onion
2 tablespoons extra-virgin olive oil
2 tablespoons chopped fresh dill
1 teaspoon dried oregano
1 cup all purpose flour
1¼ teaspoons salt
½ teaspoon coarsely ground black pepper

8 tablespoons (about) olive oil

Mix tomatoes, onion, 2 tablespoons extra-virgin olive oil, 1 tablespoon dill, and oregano in large bowl. Let stand 30 minutes. Mix in flour, salt, and pepper. Let stand until batter becomes moist, about 1 hour.

Preheat oven to 300°F. Heat 6 tablespoons oil in large skillet over medium-high heat. Drop 1 heaping tablespoon batter into oil. Repeat, forming 8 fritters total. Using slotted spatula, flatten each to 2-inch-diameter round. Cook fritters until brown, about 3 minutes per side. Transfer to paper towels to drain. Transfer to baking sheet and place in oven to keep warm. Repeat with remaining batter in 2 more batches, adding more oil to skillet as necessary. Arrange fritters on platter. Sprinkle with remaining 1 tablespoon dill.

MAKES 24

Artichokes with Basil Mayonnaise

1 cup mayonnaise
¼ cup chopped fresh basil
1 tablespoon fresh lemon juice
1 garlic clove, minced

6 10-ounce artichokes, tips of leaves trimmed

Mix first 4 ingredients in medium bowl. Season with salt and pepper.

Cook artichokes, covered, in large pot of boiling salted water until tender when pierced with knife, about 45 minutes. Drain well. (*Basil mayonnaise and artichokes can be prepared 1 day ahead. Cover separately and refrigerate.*)

Serve artichokes warm, at room temperature, or chilled with basil mayonnaise.

6 SERVINGS

Country Bread Topped with Garden Vegetables

8 ½-inch-thick slices country bread, cut crosswise in half
1 garlic clove
  Extra-virgin olive oil

3 medium tomatoes, diced
1 large yellow bell pepper, diced
6 green onions, thinly sliced
2 small zucchini, diced
12 radishes, thinly sliced
3 celery stalks, minced
¼ cup extra-virgin olive oil
¼ cup balsamic vinegar
2 tablespoons chopped fresh cilantro
½ cup almonds, toasted, chopped
  Oil-cured black olives

Prepare barbecue or preheat broiler. Grill or broil bread until lightly toasted. Rub bread with garlic and brush with oil.

Mix tomatoes and next 8 ingredients in bowl. Season to taste with salt and pepper. Spoon mixture over bread. Sprinkle with almonds. Garnish with olives.

8 SERVINGS

Crab-Filled Deviled Eggs

    8 large hard-boiled eggs, peeled
    3 tablespoons mayonnaise
 1½ tablespoons chopped fresh tarragon
    1 tablespoon minced shallot
    2 teaspoons fresh lemon juice
 ⅛ teaspoon cayenne pepper
 ¼ teaspoon hot pepper sauce
    8 ounces crabmeat

     Fresh tarragon sprigs (optional)

Cut eggs lengthwise in half. Scoop out yolks. Place yolks from 4 eggs
in medium bowl (reserve remaining yolks for another use). Mash
yolks with fork. Mix in mayonnaise, chopped tarragon, minced shallot, lemon juice, cayenne, and hot pepper sauce. Mix in crab. Season
to taste with salt and pepper.

   Mound crab mixture in cavity of each egg-white half (about 1 heaping tablespoon for each). *(Can be prepared 4 hours ahead. Cover and
refrigerate.)* Place crab-stuffed deviled eggs on platter. Garnish each
with small tarragon sprig, if desired, and serve.

MAKES 16

Spinach Dip with Feta Cheese

5 tablespoons extra-virgin olive oil

1 6-ounce bag baby spinach leaves

1 cup crumbled feta cheese

¾ cup sour cream

1 teaspoon minced garlic

½ teaspoon grated lemon peel

Purchased breadsticks

Assorted vegetables (such as carrots and Belgian endive, and blanched broccoli florets and asparagus)

Heat 1 tablespoon oil in heavy large skillet over medium-high heat. Add spinach; toss until wilted but still bright green, 3 minutes. Transfer to sieve; press out liquid. Turn out spinach onto work surface; chop coarsely. Combine 4 tablespoons oil, feta, sour cream, garlic, and peel in processor; blend until smooth. Transfer to bowl; mix in spinach. Season with salt and pepper. *(Can be made 1 day ahead. Cover; chill. Bring to room temperature before serving.)*

Place bowl with dip on platter. Serve with breadsticks and vegetables.

MAKES ABOUT 1½ CUPS

Parsley, Garlic, and Onion Spread

1 large russet potato, peeled, cubed

3 4x3x1-inch slices day-old French bread, crusts trimmed, cubed

½ cup water

3 tablespoons fresh lemon juice

1 tablespoon red wine vinegar

2 cups (packed) fresh Italian parsley

1 small white onion, quartered

1 large garlic clove, halved

2 tablespoons drained capers

⅓ cup extra-virgin olive oil

Baguette slices

Cook potato in medium saucepan of boiling salted water until tender, about 20 minutes. Drain. Return to pan and mash until smooth. Transfer ¾ cup mashed potato to large bowl.

Place bread in medium bowl. Add ½ cup water, lemon juice, and vinegar. Let stand 10 minutes to soften. Blend bread, parsley, onion, garlic, and capers in processor to smooth paste. Mix into mashed potato in large bowl. Mix in oil. Season with salt and pepper. Cover; chill at least 3 hours or overnight. Serve with baguette slices.

6 TO 8 SERVINGS

Stuffed Crimini Mushrooms

24 large crimini mushrooms or white mushrooms (each about
    2½ inches in diameter)
6 tablespoons (¾ stick) butter, room temperature
2 shallots, finely chopped
½ cup finely chopped leek (white and pale green parts only)
3 garlic cloves, finely chopped
1 tablespoon chopped fresh thyme
1 cup fresh breadcrumbs made from crustless French bread
3 tablespoons whipping cream
2 large egg yolks
½ cup grated mozzarella cheese
⅔ cup grated Parmesan cheese

    Assorted toppings (such as fresh chives, prosciutto, Kalamata olives,
       sun-dried tomatoes, goat cheese, and pistachios)

Remove stems from mushrooms, forming cavities. Chop stems finely. Spread 2 tablespoons butter over bottom of 15x10x2-inch glass baking dish. Arrange mushroom caps, rounded side down, in prepared dish. Melt remaining 4 tablespoons butter in heavy large skillet over medium-high heat. Add mushroom stems, shallots, leek, garlic, and thyme. Sauté until stems are tender, about 5 minutes. Mix in breadcrumbs; stir 5 minutes longer. Season stuffing with salt and pepper. Whisk cream and egg yolks in small bowl to blend; mix into stuffing. Sprinkle mozzarella cheese in cavities of mushroom caps. Mound stuffing in caps; top with Parmesan cheese. (*Can be prepared 1 day ahead. Cover and refrigerate.*)

Preheat oven to 375°F. Press toppings onto mushrooms. Bake uncovered until tender and heated through, about 18 minutes.

10 SERVINGS

Tamarind-Glazed Lamb Skewers with Dried-Apricot Relish

GLAZE

- ½ cup seedless unsweetened tamarind paste*
- ½ cup fresh orange juice
- ⅓ cup mild-flavored (light) molasses
- 1 teaspoon dried crushed red pepper
- 3 tablespoons fresh lime juice

APRICOT RELISH

- 2 cups chopped dried apricots
- 6 tablespoons fresh lemon juice
- ⅓ cup chopped fresh cilantro
- 2 tablespoons minced seeded red jalapeño chilies
- 2 tablespoons (packed) golden brown sugar
- 2 tablespoons cracked coriander seeds

- 2 pounds boneless leg of lamb, cut into ½-inch pieces; or 4 pounds lamb shoulder chops, fat trimmed, meat cut into ½-inch pieces
- 1 large red onion, cut into ½-inch cubes
- 20 (about) 12-inch metal skewers

FOR GLAZE: Bring first 4 ingredients to boil in small saucepan over high heat. Reduce heat and simmer until reduced to 1 cup, stirring occasionally, about 8 minutes. Remove from heat. Stir in lime juice.

FOR APRICOT RELISH: Mix apricots and next 5 ingredients in medium bowl to blend. Season with salt and pepper. (*Glaze and relish can be made 1 day ahead; cover separately and chill. Bring relish to room temperature. Stir glaze over medium heat until heated through.*)

Thread lamb and onion pieces onto skewers, using about 6 onion and lamb pieces per skewer. (*Skewers can be prepared 1 day ahead. Cover and refrigerate.*)

Prepare barbecue (medium-high heat). Sprinkle skewers with salt and pepper. Grill lamb to desired doneness, turning once and basting with glaze during last minute of grilling, about 2 minutes total for medium-rare. Transfer skewers to platter. Serve with relish.

Available at Middle Eastern, Indian, and some Asian markets.

6 SERVINGS

Cocktail Party for 12

Mojitos
(page 40)

Wine, Beer, and Mixed Drinks

Tamarind-Glazed Lamb Skewers with Dried-Apricot Relish
(at left; pictured opposite; double recipe)

Smoked Salmon Rolls with Crème Fraîche
(page 12)

Antipasto Platter

Crisp Olive Oil Pancakes with Cheese
(page 22)

Purchased Dip with Crudités

Fresh Fruit

Steamed Mussels in Thai Curry Sauce

2   13.5-ounce cans unsweetened coconut milk* (3½ cups)
1   teaspoon Thai red curry paste**
1   cup low-salt chicken broth
½   cup (packed) fresh basil leaves
2   stalks lemongrass,** trimmed, coarsely chopped (about ⅓ cup) or 1 tablespoon grated lemon peel
¼   cup fresh lime juice
2   tablespoons fish sauce (nam pla)**
3   kaffir lime leaves or 3 tablespoons fresh lime juice plus 1½ teaspoons grated lime peel

2   tablespoons peanut oil
3   pounds mussels, scrubbed, debearded
4   plum tomatoes, diced (about 1 cup)
½   cup chopped fresh cilantro

Bring coconut milk to boil in heavy large saucepan. Reduce heat to medium; add curry paste and whisk until dissolved. Add next 6 ingredients. Simmer uncovered 10 minutes. Strain curry sauce into bowl.

Heat peanut oil in large deep skillet over high heat. Add mussels. Sauté 2 minutes. Add strained curry sauce. Cover and cook until mussels open, about 4 minutes (discard any mussels that do not open). Transfer mussels and sauce to large serving bowl. Sprinkle with tomatoes and cilantro and serve.

*Available at Indian, Southeast Asian, and Latin American markets as well as many supermarkets.
**Available at Asian markets and in the Asian foods section of some supermarkets.

6 TO 8 SERVINGS

Crisp Olive Oil Pancakes with Cheese

2½   cups (or more) all purpose flour
1   teaspoon salt
¼   cup olive oil
1   large egg, beaten to blend
¾   cup warm water

    Additional olive oil
2   cups (about) grated Manchego or pecorino Romano cheese

Stir flour and salt in large bowl to blend. Using rubber spatula, mix in ¼ cup oil, then egg. Slowly stir in ¾ cup warm water to form soft dough. Knead in bowl until smooth and elastic, flouring lightly if necessary, about 5 minutes. Cover with plastic and let rest 20 minutes.

Cut dough into 4 equal pieces; cover 3 pieces with plastic. Roll out remaining piece on work surface to 13-inch rope. Cut rope into 10 equal pieces. Roll 1 piece at a time into 5-inch rope. Dip fingers in oil and flatten rope to 1-inch-wide ribbon. Roll ribbon tightly into coil. Stand coil up on 1 end. Flatten slightly and roll out coil to 3-inch-diameter round. Cover round with plastic. Repeat with remaining dough, covering rounds with plastic to prevent drying.

Pour enough oil into heavy large saucepan to reach depth of ½ inch. Attach deep-fry thermometer to side of pan; heat oil to 350°F. Fry dough rounds in batches until golden brown, about 1½ minutes per side. Transfer pancakes to paper towels to drain. Sprinkle warm pancakes with cheese. Serve warm or at room temperature.

MAKES ABOUT 40

Spicy Roasted Vegetable Soup with Toasted Tortillas

AROMATIC SOUP BASE

  2 pounds large plum tomatoes (about 10)

  2 medium onions (about 14 ounces), peeled, halved

  1 ½x3-inch strip from Mexican cinnamon stick or 1½-inch piece regular cinnamon stick

  6 whole black peppercorns

  4 large garlic cloves, unpeeled

  1 large jalapeño chili

  2 5½-inch corn tortillas, cut in half

  2 teaspoons chopped canned chipotle chilies*

Preheat broiler. Line baking sheet with heavy-duty foil. Place tomatoes close together on prepared sheet. Broil close to heat source until blackened in spots, turning once with tongs, about 2 minutes per side. Transfer tomatoes to plate and cool. Place onion halves close together on same sheet. Broil until surfaces are charred, turning once with tongs, about 4 minutes per side. Set aside and cool.

    Heat cast-iron skillet over medium-high heat 2 minutes. Using tongs, place cinnamon strip, peppercorns, garlic cloves, and jalapeño chili in hot skillet. Toast until fragrant and charred, turning and stirring occasionally, about 2 minutes for cinnamon and peppercorns and 8 minutes for garlic and jalapeño (**step 1**). Transfer all to plate. Place tortilla halves in same hot skillet. Toast until browned in spots and crisp, pressing often with spatula, about

3 minutes per side. Transfer tortillas to plate; cool, then break into very small pieces.

Peel, halve, and seed broiled tomatoes (**step 2**). Cut away most of charred surface from broiled onions and then chop. Peel garlic cloves. Stem, quarter, seed, and devein jalapeño chili. Place tomatoes, onions, garlic, jalapeño chili, and chipotle chilies in processor.

Finely grind cinnamon, peppercorns, and toasted tortillas in spice mill or coffee grinder; add to processor. Blend soup base until smooth, about 5 minutes.

Step 1. Char the aromatics—garlic, cinnamon, black peppercorns, and chili—in a hot cast-iron skillet to add smoky flavor to the soup base.

FINISHING SOUP

    3   tablespoons olive oil
 1¼   teaspoons dried oregano
    1   teaspoon ground cumin
    5   cups water
    1   1½-pound butternut squash, peeled, halved, seeded, cut into
          ½- to ¾-inch cubes
  ¾   pound red-skinned potatoes, peeled, cut into ½- to ¾-inch cubes
    1   teaspoon (or more) salt
    1   15- to 16-ounce can garbanzo beans (chickpeas), undrained
  ¼   pound green beans, trimmed, cut into 1-inch pieces
    1   cup corn kernels, cut from 1 large ear (**step 3**) or frozen
  ⅓   cup (packed) chopped fresh cilantro

        Additional 5½-inch corn tortillas

        Lime wedges

Step 2. After the charred tomatoes have cooled, peel them, halve them crosswise, and spoon out the seeds.

Step 3. To remove the kernels from an ear of corn, position a large chef's knife close to the cob and slice downward, cutting as close to the base of the kernels as possible.

Heat oil in heavy large pot over medium-high heat 2 minutes. Add soup base from processor, oregano, and cumin. Cook (sear) until base thickens enough to leave path when spoon is drawn through, stirring occasionally, about 10 minutes (**step 4**). Add 5 cups water, squash, potatoes, and 1 teaspoon salt; bring soup to boil. Reduce heat to medium, cover, and simmer until vegetables are almost tender, about 15 minutes. Add garbanzo beans with liquid, green beans, and corn. Cover; simmer until all vegetables are tender, about 5 minutes longer. Mix in cilantro; season with pepper and more salt, if desired.

Toast tortillas directly over gas flame or electric burner until browned in spots but still soft, about 40 seconds per side. Wrap in foil; keep warm.

Ladle soup into bowls. Serve with lime wedges and warm tortillas.

Step 4. Cook the soup base until it is thick enough to remain in place after a spoon makes a path through it.

Chipotle chilies canned in a spicy tomato sauce, sometimes called adobo, *are sold at Latin American markets, specialty foods stores, and some supermarkets.*

6 TO 8 SERVINGS

Caramelized Onion and Portobello Mushroom Soup with Goat Cheese Croutons

3 tablespoons butter

1½ pounds onions, halved, thinly sliced (about 5 cups)

4 fresh thyme sprigs

1½ pounds portobello mushrooms, stemmed, caps halved and cut crosswise into
    ¼-inch-thick strips

3 tablespoons Cognac or brandy

3 garlic cloves, minced

8 cups canned vegetable broth

1 cup dry white wine

18 1-inch-thick slices French-bread baguette, toasted

8 ounces soft fresh goat cheese, room temperature

Melt 1 tablespoon butter in heavy large pot over high heat. Add onions and thyme; sauté until onions begin to soften, about 8 minutes. Reduce heat to low; cook until onions are caramelized, stirring occasionally, about 20 minutes. Transfer onions to medium bowl.

Melt remaining 2 tablespoons butter in same pot over medium-high heat. Add mushrooms; sauté until soft, about 12 minutes. Add Cognac and garlic; stir 20 seconds. Stir in onion mixture, then broth and wine. Bring to boil. Reduce heat to low; simmer until onions are very tender, about 45 minutes. Discard thyme sprigs. Season soup with salt and pepper. *(Can be made 1 day ahead. Cool slightly; cover and chill. Bring to simmer before serving.)*

Preheat broiler. Place baguette slices on large baking sheet. Spread goat cheese on baguette slices, dividing equally. Broil goat cheese croutons until cheese begins to brown in spots, about 30 seconds. Divide soup among 6 bowls. Top with croutons and serve.

6 SERVINGS

Chilled Carrot and Cauliflower Soup

2 tablespoons (¼ stick) butter

1 tablespoon olive oil

2 medium-size white onions, chopped (about 3½ cups)

2 pounds carrots, peeled, cut into 1-inch pieces (about 5 cups)

4½ cups cauliflower florets (from 1 large head)

7½ cups (or more) low-salt chicken broth

½ teaspoon cayenne pepper

¾ cup buttermilk

6 tablespoons chopped red onion

6 tablespoons chopped green onions

2 tablespoons chopped fresh mint

2 tablespoons fresh lemon juice

½ cup sour cream

Melt butter with oil in heavy large pot over medium heat. Add chopped white onions and sauté until golden, about 10 minutes. Add carrots and cauliflower and sauté 5 minutes. Add 7½ cups chicken broth; bring to boil. Reduce heat, cover, and simmer until vegetables are very tender, about 45 minutes. Stir in cayenne pepper.

Working in batches, puree soup in blender until smooth. Transfer to large bowl. Stir in buttermilk. Thin with more broth, if desired. Season with salt and pepper. Chill 6 hours. (*Can be made 1 day ahead. Cover; keep chilled.*)

Mix red onion, green onions, mint, and lemon juice in small bowl. Season with salt and pepper. Ladle soup into 8 bowls. Top each with dollop of sour cream and 1 tablespoon onion mixture and serve.

8 SERVINGS

Chestnut and Lobster Soup

1   1¾- to 2-pound live lobster

3   cups whole milk
2   cups (or more) low-salt chicken broth
1   small bay leaf
6   fresh thyme sprigs
4   fresh parsley sprigs
3   cups vacuum-packed chestnuts* (15 to 16 ounces)

¼   cup Madeira

1   tablespoon butter

Minced fresh chives

Cook lobster in pot of boiling salted water until shell turns bright red and meat is opaque in center, about 8 minutes. Drain. Transfer lobster to large bowl; cool. Working over same bowl to catch juices, twist off claws. Cut off tail. Cut lobster meat from shells. Reserve lobster shells; scrape out green tomalley and discard. Cut meat into ½-inch pieces; cover and refrigerate.

Bring milk, 2 cups broth, bay leaf, thyme, parsley, and lobster shells with any accumulated juices to simmer in heavy large saucepan. Cover; simmer 10 minutes. Strain into large bowl. Return strained liquid to pan. Add chestnuts; bring to boil. Reduce heat; simmer uncovered until tender, stirring occasionally, about 15 minutes. Working in batches, puree soup in blender. (*Lobster and soup can be made 1 day ahead. Cover separately and chill.*)

Bring soup to simmer. Stir in Madeira. Thin with more broth, if necessary, and stir until heated through. Season with salt and pepper.

Meanwhile, melt butter in small skillet over medium heat. Add lobster meat; sauté 1 minute to heat through.

Ladle soup into bowls. Top with lobster meat. Sprinkle with minced fresh chives and serve.

Available at specialty foods stores and some supermarkets.

6 SERVINGS

Santa Fe Clam Chowder

- 2 tablespoons extra-virgin olive oil
- 4 ounces Spanish chorizo* or andouille sausage, cut into ⅓-inch dice
- 12 ounces white-skinned potatoes, peeled, cut into ½-inch cubes
- 1 medium onion, chopped
- 1 celery stalk, chopped
- ⅓ cup canned diced green chilies
- 1 large jalapeño chili, seeded, chopped
- 1 garlic clove, minced
- 1 teaspoon dried oregano
- 1 teaspoon ground cumin
- 1 cup canned crushed tomatoes with added puree
- 1 cup frozen white corn kernels
- 3 8-ounce bottles clam juice

- 24 littleneck clams, scrubbed
- 6 tablespoons chopped fresh cilantro

Heat oil in heavy large pot over medium-high heat. Add chorizo; sauté until fat is rendered, about 3 minutes. Add next 6 ingredients; sauté until onion begins to soften, about 5 minutes. Mix in oregano and cumin, then tomatoes, corn, and bottled clam juice. Bring to boil. Reduce heat to medium-low. Cover and simmer until potatoes are almost tender, about 12 minutes. (*Can be made 1 day ahead. Refrigerate uncovered until cool, then cover and chill. Bring to simmer before continuing.*)

Add clams to mixture in pot; cover and cook over medium-high heat until clams open and potatoes are tender, about 7 minutes (discard any clams that do not open). Mix in 4 tablespoons cilantro. Season with salt and pepper. Divide clams among 6 shallow soup bowls. Ladle chowder over. Sprinkle with remaining cilantro and serve.

A smoked-pork link sausage flavored with garlic and spices, but milder than Mexican chorizo. It is sold at Spanish markets and specialty foods stores.

6 SERVINGS

Updated Meat-and-Potatoes Dinner for 4

Santa Fe Clam Chowder
(*at left*)

Steak with Garlic and Herbs
(*page 52*)

Mashed Potatoes with Fontina and Italian Parsley
(*page 145*)

Sautéed Mixed Vegetables

Cabernet Sauvignon

Bread Pudding with Currants and Caramel
(*page 210*)

Yellow Tomato Gazpacho with Cilantro Oil and Avocado

1¾ pounds yellow tomatoes, halved
1 cup chopped seeded peeled cucumber
1 cup chopped yellow bell pepper

½ cup finely chopped onion
½ cup orange juice
3 tablespoons extra-virgin olive oil
2 tablespoons Champagne vinegar or white wine vinegar
2 garlic cloves, chopped
1 medium jalapeño chili with seeds, chopped (about 1 tablespoon)

Cilantro Oil (see recipe below)
1 avocado, peeled, pitted, chopped

Squeeze tomato juices and seeds into strainer set over bowl. Press on seeds to extract all juice. Chop tomatoes. Set aside ½ cup chopped tomatoes, ¼ cup cucumber, and ¼ cup bell pepper.

Combine remaining tomatoes, cucumber, and bell pepper in processor. Add tomato juices, onion, and next 5 ingredients; process until smooth. Season with salt and pepper. Transfer soup to bowl; add reserved vegetables. Cover; chill overnight.

Divide soup among 6 bowls. Drizzle with cilantro oil. Sprinkle with chopped avocado.

6 SERVINGS

Cilantro Oil

2 cups coarsely chopped fresh cilantro leaves and tender stems
¾ cup olive oil
2 green onions, chopped
1 medium jalapeño chili with seeds, chopped (about 1 tablespoon)
2 garlic cloves, chopped
¼ cup water

Combine all ingredients except water in processor. Puree until almost smooth. Transfer puree to fine strainer set over bowl. Using rubber spatula, press on solids to extract as much liquid as possible; discard solids in strainer. Whisk ¼ cup water into mixture in bowl. Season to taste with salt and pepper. (*Can be made 1 day ahead. Cover and refrigerate. Rewhisk before using.*)

MAKES ABOUT 1¼ CUPS

Fava Bean Soup with Carrot Cream

SOUP

1½ pounds fava bean pods (to yield ¾ cup beans)

2 tablespoons vegetable oil

1 onion, chopped

1 8-ounce Yukon Gold potato, peeled, cut into ½-inch pieces

1 medium carrot, peeled, thinly sliced

2 14-ounce cans vegetable broth

1½ cups water

¼ cup dry white wine

3 tablespoons chopped fresh parsley

⅓ cup whipping cream

CARROT CREAM

2 carrots, peeled, grated (about 1¼ cups)

⅔ cup whipping cream

1 teaspoon sugar

¼ teaspoon salt

FOR SOUP: Cook fava beans in large pot of boiling salted water 5 minutes. Drain. Cool. Cut off tip of each pod and squeeze beans into medium bowl. Peel skin from each bean (to yield about ¾ cup beans).

Heat oil in large pot over medium heat. Add onion and sauté until tender, about 10 minutes. Add beans, potato, carrot, broth, 1½ cups water, and wine. Cover and simmer until vegetables are soft, about 15 minutes. Cool slightly. Stir in parsley. Working in batches, puree soup in blender. Return to pot. Stir in cream. Season with salt and pepper. (*Soup can be made 1 day ahead; cover and chill.*)

FOR CARROT CREAM: Puree all ingredients in blender. Transfer to bowl. Chill at least 15 minutes and up to 3 hours.

Strain carrot cream into medium bowl, pressing on solids to extract as much liquid as possible. Using electric mixer, beat carrot cream until soft peaks form. Bring soup to simmer. Ladle into bowls. Top with dollop of carrot cream.

6 SERVINGS

Chive and Cucumber Vichyssoise

  1 tablespoon butter
  2 leeks (white and pale green parts only), sliced (about 2 cups)
2¼ cups canned vegetable broth
  1 6-ounce russet potato, peeled, cut into 1-inch pieces
  ½ cup whipping cream
  1 8-ounce cucumber, peeled, seeded, cut into ½-inch pieces (1⅓ cups)
  1 cup chopped fresh chives

  2 large radishes, cut into matchstick-size strips (optional)

Melt butter in heavy medium saucepan over medium heat. Add leeks; sauté just until soft but not yet brown, about 5 minutes. Add broth and potato. Simmer until potato is very tender, about 12 minutes. Using slotted spoon, transfer potato and leeks to blender. Add half of cooking liquid and blend to coarse puree. Add cream and blend, using on/off turns. Transfer to large bowl. Combine cucumber, chives, and remaining cooking liquid in blender; puree. Mix into leek puree. Season with salt and pepper. Chill at least 4 hours and up to 6 hours.

Stir soup and ladle into bowls. Garnish with radishes, if desired.

4 SERVINGS

Lunch in the Garden for 6

Fava Bean Soup with Carrot Cream
(opposite)

Spring Vegetable Paella
(page 104)

Sauvignon Blanc or Iced Tea

Lemon Charlottes with Lemon Curd and Candied Lemon Peel
(page 188)

Tangerine Margaritas

3½ cups fresh tangerine juice
1 cup tequila
½ cup Cointreau or other orange
    liqueur
6 tablespoons fresh lime juice
    Ice cubes
    Lime wedges or slices

Combine tangerine juice, tequila, Cointreau, and lime juice in large pitcher. Fill 8 double old-fashioned glasses with ice cubes. Pour tangerine mixture into glasses. Garnish with lime wedges or slices.

8 SERVINGS

Hot Chocolate with Vanilla Whipped Cream

½ vanilla bean, split lengthwise
½ cup sugar

5 cups milk
4 ounces bittersweet (not unsweetened) or semisweet chocolate, chopped
¼ cup powdered sugar
2 teaspoons unsweetened cocoa powder
1 teaspoon vanilla extract

½ cup chilled whipping cream

Using small sharp knife, scrape seeds from vanilla bean into small bowl; reserve bean. Add ½ cup sugar to seeds; rub with fingertips to distribute seeds. Set aside.

Heat 4½ cups milk and scraped vanilla bean in large saucepan over medium heat until hot. Mix in chopped chocolate and ⅓ cup vanilla sugar. Whisk until chocolate melts and mixture is smooth. Mix ½ cup milk, powdered sugar, and cocoa in small bowl. Stir into hot chocolate. Bring just to simmer, whisking often. Remove from heat and stir in vanilla.

Using electric mixer, beat cream and remaining vanilla sugar in medium bowl to soft peaks. Divide hot chocolate among 6 mugs. Top each with whipped cream.

6 SERVINGS

Campari Champagne Cocktail

4½ tablespoons honey
4½ tablespoons Campari
¾ cup fresh orange juice
1 750-ml bottle Champagne, chilled
6 small strawberries (optional)

Stir honey and Campari in 2-cup measuring cup until honey dissolves. Stir in orange juice. Cover and chill until cold, at least 30 minutes and up to 4 hours.

Pour 3 tablespoons Campari mixture into each of 6 chilled Champagne flutes. Fill glasses with Champagne. Garnish with strawberries, if desired.

6 SERVINGS

Pear and Ginger Martinis

3 cups pear nectar
1½ cups vodka
1½ tablespoons fresh lemon juice
1½ teaspoons fresh ginger juice
Ice cubes
Pear slices

Mix pear nectar, vodka, lemon juice, and ginger juice in large pitcher. Add enough ice to pitcher to fill; stir to chill. Pour into glasses. Garnish Martinis with pear slices.

8 SERVINGS

Bourbon-Ginger Ale Coolers

Ice cubes
20 tablespoons bourbon (about 1¼ cups)
7½ cups ginger ale

Place ice cubes in each of 10 glasses. Add 2 tablespoons bourbon, then ¾ cup ginger ale to each glass; stir and serve.

10 SERVINGS

Banana Yogurt Smoothie with Honey

1 large banana, peeled, sliced, frozen
1 cup chilled orange juice
½ cup plain nonfat yogurt
4 ice cubes
1 tablespoon honey

Combine all ingredients in blender. Blend until smooth. Divide smoothie between 2 glasses and serve immediately.

2 SERVINGS

Passion Fruit Mimosas

6 tablespoons fresh passion fruit juice or passion fruit blend nectar
1 cup chilled brut Champagne (about ⅔ of 375-ml bottle)
2 tablespoons Grand Marnier
Orange peel twists (optional)

Divide fruit juice between 2 Champagne flutes. Slowly pour Champagne into flutes, dividing equally. Add 1 tablespoon Grand Marnier to each flute; stir gently. Garnish with orange peel twists, if desired.

2 SERVINGS

Double-Raspberry Malt

  1 6-ounce basket fresh raspberries
¼ cup whole milk
¼ cup malted milk powder
  1 tablespoon sugar
  1 cup vanilla ice cream
  1 small scoop raspberry sorbet

Set aside 4 raspberries for garnish. Combine remaining raspberries, milk, malted milk powder, and sugar in blender; blend until smooth. Add ice cream; blend until smooth, stopping once or twice to scrape down sides of blender, if necessary. Pour into fluted soda-fountain-style glasses. Top with sorbet. Garnish malt with reserved berries.

2 SERVINGS

Post-Hike Breakfast for 4

Banana Yogurt Smoothie with Honey
(*opposite; double recipe*)

Omelets Filled with Bell Pepper, Ham, and Tomato

Sports Bars with Dried Fruit and Peanut Butter
(*page 226*)

Coffee or Tea

Mojitos

    2 cups (packed) fresh mint leaves
1⅓ cups sugar
1⅓ cups fresh lime juice (from about 18 large limes)
    4 cups light rum
        Ice cubes
    3 cups club soda

Combine mint, sugar, and lime juice in large bowl; mash well with potato masher. Let mixture stand at least 15 minutes and up to 2 hours. Stir in rum. Using ladle, divide mixture among 16 tall glasses. Fill glasses almost to top with ice cubes, then top each with 3 tablespoons club soda.

16 SERVINGS

Orange Blossom Cocktail

- 10 tablespoons fresh orange juice, chilled
- 10 tablespoons Grand Marnier or other orange liqueur, chilled
- 10 tablespoons mandarin-flavored vodka (such as Absolut Mandarin), chilled
- 2½ teaspoons orange flower water*
- 5 cups Champagne or sparkling wine (from two 750-ml bottles), chilled
- 10 orange peel strips (optional)

Pour 1 tablespoon orange juice, 1 tablespoon Grand Marnier, and 1 tablespoon vodka into each of 10 Champagne flutes. For each drink, stir in ¼ teaspoon orange flower water and then fill with ½ cup Champagne. Garnish drinks with orange strips, if desired.

*A flavoring extract available at liquor stores and in the liquor or specialty foods section of some supermarkets.

10 SERVINGS

Coffee with Baileys and Frangelico

- ½ cup chilled whipping cream
- 1 tablespoon sugar

- 8 tablespoons Frangelico (hazelnut liqueur)
- 8 tablespoons Baileys Original Irish Cream
- 2⅔ cups freshly brewed strong hot coffee

Using electric mixer, beat cream and sugar in small bowl to soft peaks. (Can be made 4 hours ahead. Cover and chill.)

Pour 2 tablespoons Frangelico and 2 tablespoons Baileys liqueur into each of 4 mugs. Pour coffee over, dividing evenly. Top each with dollop of whipped cream and serve immediately.

4 SERVINGS

Baked Salmon Stuffed with
Mascarpone Spinach (page 95)

Main Courses

Meats

Poultry

Seafood

Meatless

Pasta & Pizza

Short Ribs Provençale with Crème Fraîche Mashed Potatoes

2 tablespoons (or more) olive oil
6 pounds meaty beef short ribs

1 large onion, finely chopped
1 medium carrot, finely chopped
1 celery stalk, finely chopped
12 whole garlic cloves, peeled
2 tablespoons all purpose flour
1 tablespoon dried herbes de Provence*
2 cups red Zinfandel
2½ cups canned beef broth
1 14½-ounce can diced tomatoes in juice
1 bay leaf
½ cup (about) water

24 baby carrots, peeled
½ cup Niçois olives,** pitted
3 tablespoons chopped fresh parsley
Crème Fraîche Mashed Potatoes (see recipe on next page)

Preheat oven to 325°F. Heat 2 tablespoons olive oil in heavy large ovenproof pot over medium-high heat. Sprinkle short ribs with salt and pepper. Working in batches, add short ribs to pot and brown well, turning often, about 8 minutes per batch. Using tongs, transfer short ribs to large bowl.

Pour off all but 2 tablespoons drippings from pot or add oil as necessary to measure 2 tablespoons. Add onion, chopped carrot, and celery and cook over medium-low heat until vegetables are soft, stirring frequently, about 10 minutes. Add garlic, flour, and herbes de Provence; stir 1 minute. Add wine and 2 cups broth; bring to boil over high heat, scraping up browned bits. Add tomatoes with juices and bay leaf. Return ribs and any accumulated juices to pot. If necessary, add enough water to pot to barely cover ribs. Bring to boil.

Cover pot tightly and transfer to oven. Bake until ribs are very tender, stirring occasionally, about 2 hours 15 minutes. (*Can be made 1 day ahead. Cool slightly, then refrigerate, uncovered, until cold. Cover and keep refrigerated. Bring to simmer before continuing.*)

Add remaining ½ cup broth, peeled baby carrots, and Niçois olives to pot; press carrots gently to submerge. Cover, return to oven, and continue cooking at 350°F until carrots are tender, about 15 minutes. Discard bay leaf. Transfer short ribs and carrots to platter. Tent with foil to keep warm. If necessary, boil sauce to thicken slightly. Season sauce to taste with salt and pepper. Pour sauce over short ribs. Sprinkle with chopped fresh parsley. Serve with Crème Fraîche Mashed Potatoes.

*A dried herb mixture available at specialty foods stores and in the spice section of some markets. A mix of dried thyme, basil, savory, and fennel seeds can be substituted.
**Small brine-cured black olives; available at Italian markets, specialty foods stores, and some supermarkets.

Crème Fraîche Mashed Potatoes

3½ pounds russet potatoes, peeled, quartered
⅔ cup crème fraîche or sour cream
¼ cup (½ stick) unsalted butter

Cook potatoes in large pot of boiling salted water until just tender, about 25 minutes. Drain. Return potatoes to pot. Add crème fraîche and butter; mash until smooth. Season with salt and pepper. (*Potatoes can be made 2 hours ahead. Let stand at room temperature. Rewarm over low heat, stirring frequently.*)

6 SERVINGS

Herb-Crusted Flank Steak with Cherry Tomatoes and Olives

STEAK

- 2 tablespoons chopped fresh thyme
- 2 tablespoons chopped fresh rosemary
- 1 tablespoon chopped fresh tarragon
- 2 garlic cloves, minced
- 2 teaspoons salt
- 1½ teaspoons ground black pepper
- 2 1½-pound flank steaks
- 1 tablespoon olive oil

TOMATOES

- 2 cups halved cherry tomatoes
- 1 cup chopped fresh Italian parsley
- ¼ cup coarsely chopped pitted Kalamata olives or other brine-cured black olives
- ¼ cup coarsely chopped pitted brine-cured green olives
- ¼ cup chopped fresh basil
- ¼ cup extra-virgin olive oil
- 2 tablespoons Sherry wine vinegar

FOR STEAK: Mix first 6 ingredients in small bowl. Place steaks in large glass baking dish. Brush steaks with olive oil. Rub with herb mixture. Cover with plastic wrap and refrigerate at least 1 hour and up to 8 hours.

FOR TOMATOES: Mix all ingredients in large bowl. Season tomatoes to taste with salt and pepper. *(Can be made 2 hours ahead. Let stand at room temperature.)*

Prepare barbecue (medium-high heat). Grill steaks until cooked to desired doneness, about 4 minutes per side for medium. Transfer steaks to cutting board. Cover with aluminum foil. Let steaks stand 5 minutes.

Cut steaks across grain into ½-inch-thick slices. Arrange steak slices on large platter. Spoon tomatoes with juices over steaks and serve.

6 SERVINGS

Sun-Dried-Tomato Burgers with Balsamic Onions

    3 pounds ground beef
1⅓ cups chopped drained sun-dried tomatoes packed in oil,
        6 tablespoons oil reserved
    ½ cup grated onion
    3 tablespoons dried basil
    2 teaspoons ground cumin
    ½ teaspoon salt
    ¼ teaspoon ground black pepper

    3 onions, halved, thinly sliced
    ¼ cup balsamic vinegar

    8 hamburger buns, toasted

Line large baking sheet with parchment paper. Mix ground beef, chopped sun-dried tomatoes, 2 tablespoons reserved tomato oil, grated onion, dried basil, ground cumin, ¹/₂ teaspoon salt, and ¹/₄ teaspoon pepper in large bowl. Form mixture into 8 patties. Transfer patties to prepared baking sheet. Cover with plastic wrap and refrigerate at least 1 hour. (Can be prepared 4 hours ahead. Keep chilled.)

Prepare barbecue (medium-high heat). Heat remaining 4 tablespoons reserved tomato oil in heavy large skillet over medium-high heat. Add sliced onions and sauté until soft and starting to brown, about 10 minutes. Add balsamic vinegar. Sprinkle with salt and pepper. Simmer until onions are deep brown, stirring occasionally, about 10 minutes. Remove from heat. (Can be made 1 hour ahead. Let stand at room temperature. Wrap in foil and reheat on grill 10 minutes before serving.)

Grill burgers until cooked through, about 5 minutes per side. Place 1 burger on bottom half of each bun. Top with onions and bun tops.

8 SERVINGS

Hickory-Grilled Rib-Eye Steaks with Bacon-Molasses Butter

    6 thick bacon slices
    ⅓ cup mild-flavored (light) molasses
    6 tablespoons (¾ stick) butter, room temperature

    2 cups hickory wood chips, soaked in water 30 minutes, drained
    6 rib-eye steaks (each about 1 inch thick)

Position rack in top third of oven; preheat to 375°F. Line small baking sheet with foil. Arrange bacon on foil; brush with molasses, then sprinkle with pepper. Bake until bacon is cooked through but not crisp, about 15 minutes. Transfer bacon to work surface; cool. Chop; transfer to bowl. Add butter; stir to blend. Season with salt and pepper. *(Can be made 1 day ahead. Cover; chill. Bring to room temperature before using.)*

Prepare barbecue (medium-high heat). When coals are white, spread wood chips in 8x8-inch disposable foil pan; place pan directly atop coals. Sprinkle steaks with salt and pepper. When chips are smoking, place steaks on grill. Cover; cook steaks to desired doneness, about 4 minutes per side for medium-rare. Transfer steaks to plates. Top with butter.

6 SERVINGS

Sesame Beef and Asparagus Stir-Fry

    1½ tablespoons toasted sesame seeds
    10 ounces top sirloin, thinly sliced across grain

    2 tablespoons vegetable oil
    ¾ cup sliced red onion
    8 ounces slender asparagus, trimmed, cut into 1½-inch pieces
    ⅓ cup water
    2 tablespoons hoisin sauce
    2 teaspoons oriental sesame oil

Spread sesame seeds on large plate. Sprinkle beef with salt and pepper; coat with sesame seeds.

Heat vegetable oil in heavy large skillet over high heat. Add onion; stir-fry 1 minute. Add asparagus; stir-fry until crisp-tender, 2 minutes. Add beef; stir-fry until brown, 2 minutes. Reduce heat to medium. Add water and hoisin sauce. Cook until sauce is bubbling and coats beef, stirring often, 2 minutes. Stir in sesame oil. Season with salt and pepper.

2 SERVINGS

Backyard Barbecue for 6

Hickory-Grilled Rib-Eye Steaks with Bacon-Molasses Butter
(at left)

State Fair Potato Salad
(page 159)

Tomato and Red Onion Salad

Beer and Iced Tea

Lemon-Buttermilk Ice Pops
(page 223)

Glazed Rib-Eye Roast with
Chianti Pan Vegetables

2²/₃ cups balsamic vinegar
  1 cup dry red wine (such as Chianti)
  1 tablespoon (packed) dark brown sugar

  2 pounds red-skinned baby potatoes
1½ pounds carrots, peeled, cut into 2-inch-long pieces
  2 medium onions, unpeeled, quartered lengthwise
  6 tablespoons olive oil

  1 5-pound boneless rib-eye roast, trimmed and tied,
      room temperature
⅓ cup chopped fresh Italian parsley

Combine vinegar, wine, and sugar in heavy large saucepan. Bring to boil over medium heat, stirring to dissolve sugar. Boil until syrupy and reduced to ³/₄ cup, about 25 minutes. Remove from heat. (*Balsamic glaze can be made 1 day ahead. Cover and let stand at room temperature.*)

Position 1 rack in center and 1 rack in bottom third of oven; preheat to 325°F. Toss potatoes, carrots, and onions with olive oil in large bowl to coat. Scatter vegetables on large rimmed baking sheet. Sprinkle with salt and pepper. Place on lower rack and roast vegetables 35 minutes, stirring occasionally.

Set meat on rack set in roasting pan. Sprinkle with salt and pepper. Place on center rack and roast until thermometer inserted into center registers 125°F; continue roasting vegetables until tender, about 1 hour 40 minutes. Transfer meat to cutting board; tent with foil. Let stand 10 minutes. Mix parsley into vegetables.

Cut meat into ¹/₂-inch-thick slices. Divide meat slices and vegetables among 8 plates. Drizzle lightly with balsamic glaze and serve.

8 SERVINGS

Steak with Garlic and Herbs

½ cup (1 stick) unsalted butter

6 large garlic cloves, thinly sliced

4 6- to 8-ounce beef tenderloin steaks (about 1 inch thick)

¼ cup chopped fresh oregano

¼ cup chopped fresh basil

Melt butter in heavy small saucepan over medium heat. Remove from heat. Add garlic. Season to taste with salt and pepper. Let garlic butter stand 2 hours at room temperature.

Prepare barbecue (medium-high heat). Sprinkle steaks with salt and pepper. Grill steaks to desired doneness, about 4 minutes per side for medium-rare. Place pan of garlic butter at edge of grill to rewarm.

Transfer steaks to plates. Spoon garlic butter over. Sprinkle with herbs and serve.

4 SERVINGS

Mahogany Beef Stew with Red Wine Sauce

    4 tablespoons olive oil
    3½ pounds boneless beef chuck roast, trimmed, cut into 2½-inch pieces
    3½ cups chopped onions
    2 cups Cabernet Sauvignon
    1 14.5-ounce can diced tomatoes with Italian herbs, undrained
    ½ cup hoisin sauce
    2 bay leaves

    1 pound slender carrots, peeled, cut diagonally into 1-inch lengths
    1 tablespoon cornstarch mixed with 1 tablespoon water
    2 tablespoons chopped fresh parsley

Heat 2 tablespoons oil in heavy large pot over high heat. Sprinkle meat with salt and pepper. Add meat to pot; sauté until brown on all sides, about 10 minutes. Push meat to sides of pot. Reduce heat to medium; add 2 tablespoons oil to pot. Add onions; sauté until golden brown, about 15 minutes. Mix meat into onions. Add 1 cup wine, tomatoes with juices, hoisin sauce, and bay leaves. Bring to boil.

Reduce heat to low, cover pot, and simmer 45 minutes, stirring occasionally. Add carrots and 1 cup wine. Cover; simmer 30 minutes, stirring occasionally. Uncover, increase heat to high; boil until sauce is slightly thickened, stirring occasionally, about 15 minutes longer. Reduce heat to medium, add cornstarch mixture, and simmer until sauce thickens, stirring occasionally, about 8 minutes. Discard bay leaves. Season stew with salt and pepper. *(Can be made 1 day ahead. Cool slightly. Chill uncovered until cold, then cover and keep refrigerated. Bring to simmer before serving, stirring occasionally.)* Transfer stew to large bowl. Sprinkle with parsley and serve.

6 SERVINGS

Braised Veal with Aromatic Vegetables

1½ pounds boneless veal shoulder, cut into ¾-inch cubes
2 tablespoons (¼ stick) butter
1 small fennel bulb, thinly sliced; 2 tablespoons chopped fronds reserved
8 ounces baby carrots
1 medium onion, halved lengthwise, thinly sliced
2¼ cups plus 1 tablespoon Italian-style seasoned canned chicken broth
2 teaspoons cornstarch
2 tablespoons fresh lemon juice
1 teaspoon grated lemon peel

Sprinkle veal with salt and pepper. Melt butter in heavy large pot over medium-high heat. Add veal; sauté until brown on all sides, 5 minutes. Reduce heat to medium. Add sliced fennel, carrots, and onion; sauté 5 minutes. Add 2¼ cups broth; bring to simmer. Cover pot; reduce heat to medium-low. Simmer until veal and vegetables are tender, about 20 minutes. Mix cornstarch and 1 tablespoon broth in bowl; add to stew. Increase heat; bring to boil, stirring often. Reduce heat to medium. Add lemon juice and peel; simmer 2 minutes. Stir in fennel fronds.

6 SERVINGS

Grilled Veal Chops with Grape-Walnut Chutney

4 cups seedless red grapes (about 1½ pounds), each cut in half
¼ cup red wine vinegar
3 tablespoons sugar
2 tablespoons balsamic vinegar
½ cup chopped walnuts, toasted
3 tablespoons chopped fresh Italian parsley

8 8- to 10-ounce veal rib chops (each about ¾ inch thick)
Olive oil

Fresh parsley sprigs (optional)
Grape clusters (optional)

Heat large skillet over medium-high heat. Add halved grapes and toss until beginning to warm through, about 2 minutes. Add wine vinegar, sugar, and balsamic vinegar to grapes in skillet. Cook mixture until grape juices reduce slightly, stirring occasionally, about 10 minutes. Mix in toasted walnuts and chopped fresh parsley. (*Can be prepared 4 hours ahead. Let stand at room temperature.*)

Bring chutney to boil over high heat; boil until juices thicken to syrup, about 1 minute. Season chutney with salt and pepper; transfer to bowl.

Prepare barbecue (medium-high heat) or preheat broiler. Brush veal chops on both sides with olive oil; sprinkle with salt and pepper. Grill or broil chops until cooked to desired doneness, about 4 minutes per side for medium-rare.

Transfer veal chops to platter; garnish with parsley sprigs and grape clusters, if desired. Serve chops with grape-walnut chutney.

8 SERVINGS

Veal Scallops with Bacon and Potatoes

    3 thick-cut bacon slices, chopped
    1 pound russet potatoes, peeled, cut into ½-inch cubes

 1¾   pounds veal scallops
  ½   cup all purpose flour
    2 tablespoons (¼ stick) butter
    1 cup low-salt chicken broth
  ⅓   cup dry vermouth
    2 garlic cloves, thinly sliced
    2 teaspoons chopped fresh thyme

Cook bacon in heavy large nonstick skillet over medium-high heat until crisp. Using slotted spoon, transfer bacon to bowl. Add potatoes to drippings in skillet. Cover; cook until potatoes are tender, stirring occasionally, 8 minutes. Transfer to medium bowl; cover. Reserve skillet.

Sprinkle veal with salt and pepper; coat with flour and shake off excess. Melt butter in skillet over medium-high heat. Working in batches, add veal to skillet; cook until brown, about 2 minutes per side. Transfer to platter. Add broth, vermouth, garlic, and thyme to skillet; bring to boil, scraping up browned bits. Boil until sauce is reduced to ¾ cup, about 3 minutes. Add bacon. Season with salt and pepper. Pour sauce over veal. Serve with potatoes.

4 SERVINGS

Lamb and Sausage Pie

CRUST

 2½   cups all purpose flour
  ½   teaspoon salt
    6 tablespoons chilled solid vegetable shortening, cut into ½-inch pieces
    3 tablespoons olive oil
    3 tablespoons orange juice
    4 tablespoons (about) ice water

FILLING

    2 tablespoons olive oil
    1 pound trimmed lean leg of lamb or 2 pounds lamb shoulder chops, boned, fat trimmed, cut into ½-inch pieces (about 1 pound)
    2 medium-size sweet onions (such as Vidalia or Maui), halved, thinly sliced
    2 garlic cloves, minced
  ½   cup dry white wine
  ¼   teaspoon crumbled saffron threads
    4 ounces sweet Spanish chorizo, casings removed, finely chopped

    1 large egg, beaten to blend

FOR CRUST: Blend flour and salt in processor. Add shortening; using on/off turns, cut in shortening until mixture resembles coarse meal. Gradually add olive oil, orange juice, and 3 tablespoons ice water; process mixture until moist clumps form, adding more water by teaspoonfuls if dough is dry. Gather dough together; divide in half. Form each dough half into smooth ball; flatten each into disk. Place on work surface; cover with plastic wrap. Let dough stand at room temperature while making filling.

FOR FILLING: Heat oil in heavy large skillet over high heat. Sprinkle lamb with salt and pepper. Add lamb to skillet and sauté until brown, about 4 minutes. Transfer to bowl. Add onions and garlic to skillet and sauté 2 minutes. Reduce heat to medium-low, cover, and cook until onions are very tender, stirring occasionally, about 15 minutes. Return lamb to skillet. Add white wine and saffron; simmer until liquid is reduced by half, about 4 minutes. Stir in chorizo and sauté 2 minutes. Cool filling completely.

Preheat oven to 350°F. Roll out each dough disk between 2 sheets of parchment paper to 12-inch round. Transfer 1 dough round to ungreased rimmed baking sheet. Spread lamb filling over dough round, leaving 2-inch plain border. Cover filling with second dough round. Roll up edges, pressing together to seal well. Using small sharp knife, cut small X in center of top crust to allow steam to escape. Brush crust with beaten egg.

Bake pie until crust is golden brown, about 35 minutes. Let cool 15 minutes. Serve warm or at room temperature.

6 SERVINGS

Grilled Butterflied Leg of Lamb and Vegetables with Lemon-Herb Dressing

LAMB

- ¾ cup olive oil
- 12 garlic cloves, chopped
- 2 tablespoons chopped fresh rosemary
- 2 tablespoons chopped fresh thyme
- 1½ teaspoons salt
- 1½ teaspoons coarsely ground black pepper
- 1 5- to 5½-pound leg of lamb, boned, butterflied, trimmed

DRESSING AND VEGETABLES

- 1 cup fresh lemon juice
- 5 shallots, minced
- ¾ cup olive oil
- ¾ cup chopped fresh parsley
- ½ cup chopped fresh mint
- 6 medium-size zucchini, trimmed, each quartered lengthwise

6 medium-size yellow crookneck squash, trimmed, each cut lengthwise into ⅓-inch-thick slices

3 large red bell peppers, stemmed, seeded, each cut lengthwise into 6 strips

4 medium-size red onions, peeled, halved through root end, each half cut into 3 wedges with some of core attached

2 cups red Zinfandel

Nonstick vegetable oil spray

7 ounces feta cheese, crumbled (about 1¾ cups)
Fresh rosemary, thyme, and mint sprigs

FOR LAMB: Mix first 6 ingredients in medium bowl. Place lamb in 15x10x2-inch glass baking dish. Pour marinade over. Turn lamb, spreading marinade to coat evenly on all sides. Cover dish with plastic wrap and refrigerate for 1 day, turning lamb occasionally.

FOR DRESSING AND VEGETABLES: Whisk first 5 ingredients in medium bowl to blend. Season dressing with salt and pepper.

Place zucchini, yellow squash, and red bell peppers in separate dishes. Sprinkle each lightly with salt and pepper. Spoon ⅓ cup dressing over each and turn to coat; reserve remaining dressing. Arrange red onions in large glass dish; sprinkle with salt and pepper. Pour wine over onions. Let vegetables and onions marinate at least 2 hours and up to 4 hours, basting or turning occasionally.

Spray grill rack with nonstick spray and prepare barbecue (medium-high heat). Grill vegetables in batches until just tender, turning occasionally, about 15 minutes for onions, 10 minutes for red bell peppers, and 8 minutes for zucchini and yellow squash. Transfer vegetables to baking sheets. Reserve wine from onions to baste lamb.

Place butterflied lamb on grill rack with some rosemary and thyme marinade still clinging to lamb. Grill until meat thermometer inserted into center registers 130°F for medium-rare, turning occasionally and basting with reserved wine from onions, about 35 minutes. Transfer lamb to work surface; let rest 15 minutes.

Starting at 1 corner and positioning knife at slight angle, slice lamb thinly across grain. Arrange lamb slices on large platter. Arrange grilled vegetables around lamb. Drizzle vegetables with reserved lemon-herb dressing. Sprinkle with feta cheese. Garnish with fresh rosemary, thyme, and mint sprigs.

8 TO 10 SERVINGS

Alfresco Dinner for 10

Spinach Dip with Feta Cheese
(page 18; double recipe)

Bourbon Ginger-Ale Coolers
(page 38)

Grilled Butterflied Leg of Lamb and Vegetables with Lemon-Herb Dressing
(at left; pictured opposite)

Rice Pilaf

Zinfandel

Cherry Tart
(page 175)

Braised Lamb Shanks with Ginger and Five-Spice

12 dried shiitake mushrooms
2½ cups boiling water

1 3-inch-long piece fresh ginger, peeled, thickly sliced
3 garlic cloves, peeled
¾ cup coarsely chopped fresh cilantro
4½ tablespoons black bean garlic sauce*
6 teaspoons peanut oil
1½ teaspoons Chinese five-spice powder**
6 large lamb shanks (about 1 pound each), excess fat trimmed

¾ cup thinly sliced green onions

¾ cup dry Sherry

Steamed white rice

Place mushrooms in bowl. Pour boiling water over; let soak until mushrooms soften, at least 45 minutes and up to 4 hours. Strain mixture, reserving 1½ cups soaking liquid. Cut stems from mushrooms and discard; thinly slice caps.

With food processor running, add ginger and garlic and finely chop. Add cilantro, black bean sauce, 2 teaspoons peanut oil, and five-spice powder. Process until paste forms, occasionally scraping down sides of work bowl. Using sharp knife, cut 5 small shallow slits into each lamb shank, spacing apart; rub generous 1 tablespoon black bean-cilantro paste into slits and all over surface of each shank. (*Mushrooms and lamb shanks can be prepared 6 hours ahead. Cover mushrooms, soaking liquid, and shanks separately and chill.*)

Preheat oven to 325°F. Cut six 18-inch squares of aluminum foil; place on work surface. Place green onions and sliced mushroom caps in center of each foil square, dividing equally. Heat remaining 4 teaspoons peanut oil in heavy large skillet over medium-high heat. Working in batches, add lamb shanks and cook until brown on all sides, about 5 minutes per batch. Place 1 lamb shank atop green onions and mushrooms on each foil square.

Pour reserved mushroom soaking liquid and Sherry into same skillet. Boil until liquid is reduced to ¾ cup, scraping up any browned bits from bottom of skillet, about 10 minutes. Spoon 2 tablespoons reduced liquid over each lamb shank, pulling up foil around shanks to prevent liquid from spilling out. Enclose shanks completely in foil, twisting foil to seal; place on large rimmed baking sheet.

Bake lamb shanks until very tender and meat almost falls off bones, about 2 hours. Open up foil packets; place each atop bowl of steamed rice, allowing diners to remove foil.

Available at Asian markets and in the Asian foods section of supermarkets.
**Five-spice powder is a blend of ground anise, cinnamon, star anise, cloves, and ginger; available in the spice section of most supermarkets.*

6 SERVINGS

Spiced Lamb- and Rice-Stuffed Tomatoes

  8 large firm tomatoes (each 3 to 3½ inches in diameter)
  2 tablespoons (¼ stick) butter
  1 large onion, chopped
  1 pound ground lamb
  ½ cup dry red wine
  ¼ cup chopped fresh mint
  4 tablespoons chopped fresh parsley
  ¼ teaspoon ground cinnamon
  ¾ cup cooked long-grain white rice (about ¼ cup uncooked)
  ¼ cup plain dry breadcrumbs
  ½ cup freshly grated Parmesan cheese

Preheat oven to 350°F. Cut off top third of tomatoes; chop tops and reserve. Scoop out seeds, juice, and pulp from tomatoes and discard. Melt butter in heavy large skillet over medium-high heat. Add onion; sauté until tender, 8 minutes. Add lamb; sauté until browned, 7 minutes. Add chopped tomato, wine, mint, 2 tablespoons parsley, and cinnamon. Bring to boil. Reduce heat; simmer until thick, stirring often, 12 minutes. Stir in rice. Place tomatoes in 13x9x2-inch glass baking dish. Spoon in lamb mixture. Sprinkle with breadcrumbs, then cheese. Bake until cheese begins to turn golden, about 25 minutes. Top with 2 tablespoons parsley.

8 SERVINGS

Spring Lamb with Tomato and Herb Vinaigrette

  ¼ cup chopped fresh mint
  ¼ cup chopped fresh basil
  ¼ cup chopped green onions
  2 tablespoons chopped fresh marjoram
  2 tablespoons balsamic vinegar
  1 tablespoon olive oil
  1 6½- to 7-pound bone-in leg of lamb

    Tomato and Herb Vinaigrette (see recipe on next page)

Mix first 6 ingredients in bowl. Season mixture with salt and pepper. Place lamb in large glass baking dish. Rub all over with herb mixture. Cover; chill overnight.

    Preheat oven to 450°F. Uncover lamb; transfer to rack set in large roasting pan. Roast 20 minutes. Reduce heat to 350°F. Roast until meat thermometer inserted into thickest part registers 135°F for medium, about 1 hour 15 minutes. Transfer lamb to platter. Tent with foil; let stand 20 minutes. Serve with vinaigrette.

10 SERVINGS

Tomato and Herb Vinaigrette

1¼ cups olive oil
¾ cup chopped fresh mint
⅔ cup chopped fresh basil
10 tablespoons red wine vinegar
2½ tablespoons chopped fresh marjoram
2½ tablespoons whole grain Dijon mustard
1¼ teaspoons sugar
1¼ teaspoons salt
1⅔ cups chopped seeded plum tomatoes

Whisk first 8 ingredients in bowl. Add tomatoes; season with black pepper. (*Can be prepared 2 hours ahead. Let vinaigrette stand at room temperature; mix before using.*)

MAKES ABOUT 2½ CUPS

Grilled Rack of Lamb with Rosemary and Olive Oil

3 8-rib racks of lamb (each about 1½ to 1¾ pounds), trimmed
¾ cup olive oil
3 tablespoons chopped fresh rosemary
1½ teaspoons dried crushed red pepper (optional)

3 cups applewood chips or mesquite wood chips, soaked in water 1 hour (optional)
1 8x8x1¾-inch disposable aluminum-foil pan (optional)

Place lamb in 15x10x2-inch glass baking dish. Whisk oil, rosemary, and crushed pepper (if desired) in small bowl. Pour marinade over lamb; turn to coat. Cover and chill at least 6 hours and up to 1 day, turning occasionally.

Prepare barbecue (medium-high heat). Drain marinade from lamb; sprinkle lamb on both sides with salt and pepper. If using wood chips, drain well and place in foil pan. Place pan directly atop charcoal on barbecue. When wood chips begin to smoke, place lamb on grill rack above chips. Grill lamb to desired doneness, turning occasionally, about 20 minutes for medium-rare or until meat thermometer inserted into center registers 125°F.

Transfer lamb to work surface; let rest 15 minutes. Cut lamb between bones into individual chops; arrange on platter.

8 SERVINGS

Saturday Night Dinner Party for 8

Chilled Carrot and Cauliflower Soup
(*page 28*)

Grilled Rack of Lamb with Rosemary and Olive Oil
(*at left*)

Sautéed Baby Squash and Radishes with Marjoram
(*page 138*)

Roasted New Potatoes

Côtes du Rhône

Blueberry Tartlets with Lime Curd
(*page 174*)

Pork and Hominy Stew

  1 tablespoon plus 2 teaspoons chili powder
  1 teaspoon salt
  ½ teaspoon ground black pepper
  2½ pounds boneless pork shoulder butt, cut into 2½-inch pieces or boneless country pork spareribs, cut into 2-inch pieces
  3 bacon slices, chopped

  1 large onion, thinly sliced
  1 cup diced smoked ham
  1 medium carrot, peeled, chopped
  6 large garlic cloves, chopped
  2 poblano chilies,* seeded, cut into 2x¼-inch strips
  2 cups drained canned hominy (from two 15-ounce cans)
  1 cup canned diced tomatoes in juice
  1 cup beer
  1 cup low-salt chicken broth
  1 teaspoon dried marjoram

  ¼ cup chopped fresh cilantro

Mix 1 tablespoon chili powder, salt, and pepper in bowl. Rub spice mixture all over pork. Sauté bacon in heavy large pot over medium heat until crisp, about 5 minutes. Transfer bacon to paper towels to drain. Working in batches, add pork to drippings in pot and sauté until brown on all sides, about 10 minutes per batch. Using slotted spoon, transfer pork to bowl.

Reduce heat to medium. Add onion, ham, carrot, and garlic to pot; cover and cook 5 minutes, stirring occasionally, and scraping up browned bits. Add chilies; stir 1 minute. Stir in hominy, tomatoes with juices, beer, broth, marjoram, pork, and remaining 2 teaspoons chili powder and bring to boil. Reduce heat; cover and simmer until pork is very tender, about 1 hour. (*Can be prepared 1 day ahead. Cover and refrigerate bacon. Cool stew slightly. Refrigerate uncovered until cold, then cover and keep chilled.*)

Simmer stew uncovered until liquid is slightly reduced and thickened, about 10 minutes. Season with salt and pepper. Transfer to bowl. Sprinkle with reserved bacon and cilantro.

These fresh green chilies, often called pasillas, *are available at Latin American markets and also at some supermarkets.*

4 SERVINGS

South-of-the-Border Dinner for 4

Guacamole and Tortilla Chips

Tangerine Margaritas
(*page 36*)

Pork and Hominy Stew
(*at left; pictured opposite*)

Mixed Green Salad

Dulce de Leche Ice Cream Pie with Mocha Fudge Sauce
(*page 224*)

Dijon-Glazed Ham with Roasted Pearl Onions

    2 pounds pearl onions

    1 cup (packed) dark brown sugar
    5 tablespoons balsamic vinegar
    3 tablespoons Dijon mustard
    ¼ cup (½ stick) butter, diced
    1 teaspoon salt
    ¼ teaspoon ground black pepper

    1 8- to 10-pound half ham shank, fully cooked, fat trimmed to ½-inch thickness

Cook onions in large pot of boiling salted water 2 minutes; drain. Trim root ends, leaving base intact. Peel. (*Can be made 1 day ahead. Cover and refrigerate.*)

Preheat oven to 325°F. Combine sugar, vinegar, and mustard in bowl for glaze. Transfer onions to 11x7x2-inch glass baking dish. Add ⅔ cup glaze, butter, 1 teaspoon salt, ¼ teaspoon pepper, and ½ cup water; toss to coat. Cover with foil.

Line large roasting pan with foil. Making ½-inch-deep slits, score ham with diamond pattern. Place ham in pan and roast 45 minutes. Place onions in oven. Roast ham and onions 25 minutes. Uncover onions. Continue roasting onions and ham 50 minutes.

Baste ham with some of glaze. Continue to roast ham and onions until deep brown and glazed, brushing ham with glaze every 10 minutes, about 30 minutes longer. Transfer ham to large platter. Transfer onion mixture to bowl. Serve ham, passing onion mixture separately.

12 SERVINGS

Cajun Ham Hash

    3 tablespoons (or more) olive oil
    2 cups chopped green onions
 1½ cups diced ham
    1 cup chopped bell pepper
    3 cups southern-style frozen hash brown potatoes from 32-ounce bag
 1½ tablespoons chopped fresh thyme or 2 teaspoons dried
    ¾ teaspoon Cajun or Creole seasoning

Heat 3 tablespoons oil in large nonstick skillet over medium-high heat. Add 1½ cups onions, ham, and bell pepper. Sauté until vegetables begin to soften, about 3 minutes. Add potatoes, thyme, and seasoning; stir to combine. Reduce heat to medium. Cover; cook 8 minutes. Uncover; cook until potatoes are crusty, stirring occasionally, adding more oil by tablespoonfuls if potatoes are sticking, 7 minutes longer. Mix in ½ cup onions. Season with salt and pepper.

2 SERVINGS

Grilled Spareribs with Cherry Cola Glaze

4   12-ounce cans cherry cola (flat)
2   cups cherry jam or preserves
2/3 cup Dijon mustard with horseradish
3   tablespoons soy sauce
2   tablespoons malt vinegar or apple cider vinegar
1   tablespoon hot pepper sauce

7¼ to 7½ pounds well-trimmed pork spareribs

Boil cherry cola in heavy large saucepan over medium-high heat until reduced to 1½ cups, about 45 minutes. Stir in next 5 ingredients. Reduce heat to medium and simmer until mixture is reduced to 2½ cups, stirring occasionally, about 35 minutes. Transfer glaze to large bowl. (*Can be made 1 week ahead. Cover; chill. Bring to room temperature before using.*)

Position racks in top and bottom thirds of oven and preheat to 325°F. Sprinkle ribs with salt and pepper. Wrap each rib rack tightly in foil, enclosing completely. Divide foil packets between 2 rimmed baking sheets. Bake until ribs are very tender, switching positions of baking sheets halfway through baking, about 2 hours total. Cool ribs slightly in foil. Pour off any fat from foil packets. (*Can be prepared 1 day ahead. Keep covered in foil packets and refrigerate. Let stand at room temperature 1 hour before continuing.*)

Prepare barbecue (medium-low heat). Cut each rib rack between bones into individual ribs. Set aside 1 cup glaze. Add ribs to bowl with remaining glaze and toss to coat thoroughly. Grill ribs until brown and glazed, turning to prevent burning, about 5 minutes total. Serve, passing reserved glaze separately.

6 SERVINGS

Pork Chops with Spicy Chutney Barbecue Sauce

        8 cups water
       ½ cup coarse salt
       ½ cup (packed) golden brown sugar
       ¼ cup chili powder
        8 1½-inch-thick bone-in pork rib chops

           Olive oil
           Spicy Chutney Barbecue Sauce (see recipe below)

Combine 2 cups water, salt, brown sugar, and chili powder in large nonreactive pot. Bring to boil, stirring to dissolve salt and sugar. Remove from heat. Add 6 cups cold water. Cool brine completely. Add pork chops, pressing to submerge. Cover pot; refrigerate at least 6 hours and up to 1 day.

Prepare barbecue (medium-high heat). Drain pork; pat dry with paper towels. Brush pork on both sides with oil; sprinkle with pepper. Grill pork to desired doneness, about 10 minutes per side or until instant-read thermometer registers 150°F for medium. Serve pork with Spicy Chutney Barbecue Sauce.

8 SERVINGS

Spicy Chutney Barbecue Sauce

        2 tablespoons (¼ stick) butter
        1 medium onion, finely chopped
        2 garlic cloves, minced
        1 12-ounce bottle chili sauce
        1 9- to 10-ounce jar mango chutney
       ⅓ cup apple cider vinegar
        2 tablespoons Worcestershire sauce
        2 tablespoons Dijon mustard
     1½ teaspoons hot pepper sauce (preferably habañero pepper)

Melt butter in heavy medium saucepan over medium heat. Add onion; sauté until golden, about 5 minutes. Add garlic and stir 1 minute. Stir in chili sauce, chutney, vinegar, Worcestershire sauce, and mustard; bring to boil. Reduce heat to medium-low and simmer until mixture is reduced to 2¾ cups, stirring frequently, about 10 minutes. Stir in hot pepper sauce. Transfer sauce to bowl; cool to room temperature, about 1 hour. (*Can be made 3 days ahead. Cover; chill. Bring to room temperature before serving.*)

MAKES ABOUT 2¾ CUPS

Brined Pork Loin with Onion, Raisin, and Garlic Compote

- 8 cups water
- ½ cup coarse salt
- ½ cup (packed) golden brown sugar
- 1 tablespoon fennel seeds
- 1 tablespoon coriander seeds
- 1 tablespoon whole black peppercorns
- 3 bay leaves
- 1 center-cut boneless pork loin roast (about 4 pounds)
- 1 tablespoon olive oil
- 2 teaspoons chopped fresh sage
- 2 teaspoons chopped fresh rosemary
- 2 teaspoons chopped fresh thyme
- 2 teaspoons chopped fresh marjoram

  Onion, Raisin, and Garlic Compote (see recipe on next page)

Combine first 7 ingredients in heavy large pot. Bring to simmer over medium heat, stirring to dissolve salt and sugar. Remove from heat. Cool to room temperature. Transfer brine to very large bowl. Add pork (weight pork with plate to keep below surface). Cover; refrigerate overnight. Drain pork. Return pork to bowl; cover with water (weight pork with plate). Soak at room temperature 2 hours.

Position rack in top third of oven and preheat to 350°F. Drain pork. Pat dry. Transfer to rack set in large roasting pan. Rub pork all over with oil. Sprinkle with fresh herbs, pressing to adhere. Sprinkle with pepper. Roast until thermometer inserted into center of pork registers 150°F, about 1 hour 40 minutes. Transfer pork to cutting board; tent with foil. Let stand 10 minutes.

Cut pork into ¼- to ½-inch-thick slices. Serve with compote.

8 SERVINGS

Onion, Raisin, and Garlic Compote

    1   pound pearl onions
    ¼   cup (½ stick) butter
   24   garlic cloves, peeled
    1   bay leaf
   1½   cups tawny Port
    ¼   cup white wine vinegar
    4   teaspoons sugar
    ½   teaspoon salt
    ½   cup raisins
   1½   teaspoons chopped fresh thyme

Bring large saucepan of water to boil. Add onions. Boil 2 minutes. Drain. Rinse under cold water. Peel onions. Trim root end slightly, leaving root base intact.

Melt butter in heavy medium saucepan over medium-low heat. Add garlic and bay leaf. Sauté until garlic is golden brown, about 6 minutes. Add Port, vinegar, sugar, and salt. Simmer 8 minutes. Add onions and raisins. Simmer until onions are tender, stirring occasionally, about 9 minutes. Remove from heat. Stir in thyme. Discard bay leaf. Season with salt and pepper. (*Can be made 1 day ahead. Cover and refrigerate. Rewarm over medium heat before serving.*) Serve warm.

MAKES ABOUT 2 CUPS

Hearthside Supper for 8

Cheese and Crackers

Pear and Ginger Martinis
(*page 37*)

Brined Pork Loin with Onion, Raisin, and Garlic Compote
(*at left; pictured opposite*)

Sautéed Spinach

Wild Rice

Merlot

Chocolate and Mixed-Nut Tart in Cookie Crust
(*page 176*)

Grilled Pork Tenderloin with Pipián Sauce

1 1- to 1¼-pound pork tenderloin, cut into ½-inch-thick medallions

3 tablespoons vegetable oil
½ onion, coarsely chopped
¾ cup pumpkin seeds (pepitas)
¼ cup peanuts (1½ ounces)
¼ cup sesame seeds (1½ ounces)
2 garlic cloves, minced

4 cups water
12 ounces tomatillos,* husked
2 teaspoons coarsely chopped seeded jalapeño chili
1½ cups fresh cilantro leaves
1½ cups torn romaine leaves
1¼ cups low-salt chicken broth
3 radishes, trimmed, chopped

Place pork between 2 sheets of waxed paper. Pound to ¼- to ½-inch thickness. (*Can be made 4 hours ahead. Cover; chill.*)

Heat 2 tablespoons oil in heavy large skillet over medium heat. Add next 5 ingredients. Sauté until seeds are lightly browned, about 4 minutes. Set aside.

Place 4 cups water, tomatillos, and jalapeño in small saucepan. Simmer over medium heat until tomatillos are soft and olive-green color, about 15 minutes. Drain, reserving ¼ cup cooking liquid. Transfer tomatillos, jalapeño, reserved ¼ cup liquid, cilantro, lettuce, broth, radishes, and seed mixture to blender. Blend sauce until smooth, stopping occasionally to push down ingredients.

Heat 1 tablespoon oil in large skillet over medium heat. Add sauce; cook until thickened, about 4 minutes. Season to taste with salt and pepper. (*Can be prepared 2 hours ahead. Let sauce stand at room temperature.*)

Prepare barbecue (medium-high heat). Sprinkle pork with salt and pepper. Grill until cooked through, about 2 minutes per side. Divide among 4 plates. Stir sauce over medium heat until heated through. Spoon sauce over pork.

Green tomato-like vegetables with paper-thin husks. Available at Latin American markets and some supermarkets.

4 SERVINGS

Skillet Chicken and Vegetables

- 4 chicken thighs with skin and bone
- 1 tablespoon paprika
- 2 tablespoons vegetable oil
- ¾ pound small red-skinned potatoes, halved
- 8 boiling onions, peeled
- 2 large carrots, peeled, cut into 1-inch pieces
- 1 tablespoon all purpose flour
- 1 cup low-salt chicken broth
- ½ cup dry white wine
  Chopped fresh parsley

Sprinkle chicken on all sides with paprika, salt, and pepper. Heat oil in heavy large skillet over medium-high heat. Add chicken and sauté until brown, about 3 minutes per side. Transfer chicken to plate. Add vegetables and stir 2 minutes. Sprinkle vegetables with flour and stir to coat. Gradually stir in broth and wine; bring to boil, stirring frequently. Return chicken and any juices to skillet; bring to boil. Reduce heat to medium-low. Cover and simmer until chicken is cooked through, about 30 minutes. Season with salt and pepper. Sprinkle with chopped fresh parsley and serve.

4 SERVINGS

POULTRY

Roasted Chicken with Caramelized Onions

3 heads of garlic, cloves separated and peeled
1 cup whole milk
7 tablespoons olive oil

¼ cup (½ stick) butter
4 onions, cut into 1-inch pieces
⅔ cup balsamic vinegar
2 fresh thyme sprigs
1 bay leaf
3 tablespoons whipping cream
2 whole chickens (each about 3½ pounds), split in half
¼ cup chopped fresh parsley

Preheat oven to 400°F. Bring garlic and milk to boil in heavy medium saucepan over high heat. Drain. Discard milk. Transfer garlic to 8x8x2-inch metal baking pan. Add 3 tablespoons oil and toss to coat. Roast until golden, about 13 minutes. Cool slightly. Transfer garlic with its cooking oil to processor; blend to form paste. Season with salt and pepper. *(Garlic paste can be made 1 day ahead. Cover and chill.)*

Melt butter and 1 tablespoon oil in heavy large skillet over medium-low heat. Add onions and sauté until golden brown, stirring occasionally, about 40 minutes. Add vinegar, thyme, and bay leaf. Simmer until liquid is reduced by half, about 3 minutes. Stir in cream. Season to taste with salt and pepper.

Meanwhile, preheat oven to 450°F. Heat remaining 3 tablespoons oil in heavy large nonstick skillet over high heat. Sprinkle chicken with salt and pepper. Working in 2 batches, add chicken, skin side down, to skillet and cook until skin is golden brown (do not turn), about 4 minutes. Place chicken, skin side up, on large rimmed baking sheet. Roast until chicken is cooked through and juices run clear when thigh is pierced with knife, about 20 minutes. Spread garlic paste atop chicken halves, dividing equally. Bake until golden brown, about 5 minutes longer.

Rewarm onions over medium-low heat, stirring often. Spoon onions in center of 4 plates. Place chicken halves atop onions. Sprinkle with chopped fresh parsley and serve.

4 SERVINGS

Rustic Supper for 4

Fresh Fennel Salad with Lemon and Parmesan
(page 158; halve recipe)

Roasted Chicken with Caramelized Onions
(at left)

Creamy Polenta with Gorgonzola and Spinach
(page 144)

Chardonnay

Sweet Potato Tart with Pecans and Marshmallows
(page 180)

Sausage-Stuffed Chicken Thighs on Egg Noodles

- 4 ounces (about 1 link) sweet Italian sausage, casing removed, meat crumbled
- ½ cup fresh breadcrumbs from crustless day-old French bread
- ½ cup freshly grated Parmesan cheese (about 1½ ounces)
- 1 large shallot, minced
- 1 large egg
- 2 tablespoons chopped fresh parsley
- 2 teaspoons chopped fresh thyme
- ½ teaspoon salt
- ¼ teaspoon ground black pepper
- 8 large skinless boneless chicken thighs (about 2½ pounds total)

- 2 tablespoons olive oil
- ¼ cup chopped pancetta or bacon
- ¾ cup finely chopped onion
- 6 garlic cloves, minced
- 1 750-ml bottle Chianti or other dry red wine
- 3 cups low-salt chicken broth
- 2 cups crushed tomatoes in puree
- 1 bay leaf
- 1 teaspoon dried basil

- 1 pound egg noodles

Mix first 9 ingredients in medium bowl. Place 1 chicken thigh on work surface. Fill area where bone was removed with 2 tablespoons stuffing. Wrap chicken thigh around filling and tie with kitchen string to hold together. Repeat with remaining chicken thighs and stuffing. Sprinkle generously with salt and pepper.

Heat olive oil in heavy large skillet over medium-high heat. Add pancetta; sauté until light brown and fat is rendered, about 5 minutes. Transfer pancetta to paper towels to drain. Add chicken to drippings in skillet; cook until golden on all sides, about 10 minutes. Transfer to plate. Add onion and garlic to skillet; sauté until tender, about 10 minutes. Return pancetta to skillet. Add wine; boil until mixture is reduced to 2 cups, about 12 minutes. Add broth, tomatoes, bay leaf, basil, and chicken thighs; bring to boil. Reduce heat; simmer uncovered until chicken is cooked through, about 35 minutes. (*Can be prepared 1 day ahead. Cool slightly. Refrigerate until cold, then cover and keep refrigerated. Rewarm over medium heat before continuing.*)

Transfer chicken to bowl; cover to keep warm. Simmer sauce in skillet until slightly thickened and reduced to 4 cups, about 10 minutes. Season with salt and pepper.

Meanwhile, cook noodles in large pot of boiling salted water until just tender but still firm to bite. Drain. Transfer noodles to large platter. Top with chicken and sauce and serve.

6 TO 8 SERVINGS

Lemon Chicken and Artichokes with Dill Sauce

    2 lemons, halved
    8 large artichokes

    ⅔ cup dry white wine
    ½ cup fresh lemon juice
    ⅓ cup olive oil
    12 garlic cloves, minced
    2 chickens (each about 3¾ pounds), giblets removed, each cut into 8 pieces

    3 large egg yolks
    2 tablespoons chopped fresh dill

Squeeze juice from lemons into large pot of salted water. Add lemons. Trim artichokes and cut lengthwise into quarters; add to pot. Bring to boil over medium-high heat. Cover partially and boil until artichokes are tender, about 20 minutes. Drain. Using shears, cut ½ inch off tips of leaves. Scoop out choke. (*Artichokes can be prepared 1 day ahead. Cool. Wrap tightly in plastic and refrigerate.*)

Preheat oven to 375°F. Whisk wine, lemon juice, oil, and garlic in large bowl to blend. Add chicken. Turn to coat. Let marinate 20 minutes. Remove chicken from marinade and arrange, skin side up, on large rimmed baking sheet. Reserve marinade. Bake chicken 30 minutes.

Meanwhile, add artichokes to marinade in large bowl; toss to coat. Marinate 25 minutes.

Transfer artichokes to another rimmed baking sheet; place in oven with chicken and bake 10 minutes. Pour marinade into saucepan; bring to boil. Baste chicken and artichokes with ⅓ of marinade. Continue baking until chicken is cooked through, about 15 minutes.

Using slotted spoon, transfer chicken and artichokes to platter; tent with foil.

Strain pan juices from baking sheets into 2-cup glass measuring cup. Transfer 1¼ cups pan juices to medium saucepan. Whisk in egg yolks. Whisk constantly over medium-high heat just until mixture boils and thickens, 3 minutes. Stir in dill. Season with salt and pepper.

Spoon some sauce over chicken and artichokes on platter. Serve, passing remaining sauce separately.

6 TO 8 SERVINGS

Tandoori-Spiced Chicken with Tomato-Ginger Chutney

MARINADE

- 2 cups plain yogurt
- 2 tablespoons ground coriander
- 2 tablespoons mild paprika
- 1½ tablespoons ground cumin
- 1½ tablespoons ground ginger
- 1 tablespoon garlic powder
- 1 tablespoon ground black pepper
- ½ teaspoon ground cinnamon
- ½ teaspoon ground cardamom
- ¼ teaspoon ground cloves
- 6 7- to 8-ounce skinless boneless chicken breast halves

CHUTNEY

- 3 cups chopped seeded tomatoes (about 1¼ pounds)
- ¾ cup chopped red onion
- ½ cup chopped fresh mint
- 3 tablespoons minced peeled fresh ginger
- 3 tablespoons fresh lime juice

FOR MARINADE: Whisk yogurt and next 9 ingredients in large bowl to blend. Add chicken; turn to coat. Cover and chill overnight.

FOR CHUTNEY: Combine all ingredients in medium bowl. Season to taste with salt and pepper. *(Can be made 1 day ahead. Cover and chill.)*

Prepare barbecue (medium-high heat). Brush grill with oil. Transfer marinade-coated chicken to barbecue grill. Grill chicken until cooked through, about 7 minutes per side. Transfer chicken to cutting board. Cut crosswise on diagonal into ½-inch-thick slices. Transfer to platter. Serve with chutney.

6 SERVINGS

Hoisin-Glazed Chicken Wraps

1 tablespoon oriental sesame oil
1 pound skinless boneless chicken breast halves, cut into 2-inch-long strips
4 garlic cloves, minced
2 bunches green onions, cut into 1-inch pieces (about 3 cups)
½ cup (about) hoisin sauce

6 8-inch-diameter flour tortillas

2 cups thinly sliced romaine or iceberg lettuce
6 tablespoons chopped fresh cilantro

Heat oil in large nonstick skillet over medium-high heat. Add chicken and garlic and sauté 2 minutes. Add green onions and sauté until chicken is cooked through, about 1½ minutes longer. Stir in 2 tablespoons hoisin sauce. Remove from heat.

Wrap tortillas in paper towels and heat in microwave on high 1 minute. (Or heat each tortilla in dry skillet over medium heat 1 minute per side.)

Brush each warm tortilla lightly with some of remaining hoisin sauce. Sprinkle lettuce and cilantro over hoisin. Spoon chicken mixture in center of tortillas. Roll up and serve.

6 SERVINGS

Chicken with Prosciutto, Rosemary, and White Wine

2 tablespoons extra-virgin olive oil
3 large chicken breast halves with ribs and skin, cut crosswise in half
3 chicken drumsticks with skin
3 chicken thighs with skin
1 cup ¼-inch cubes prosciutto (about 5 ounces)
6 garlic cloves, thinly sliced
2 tablespoons chopped fresh rosemary
1¼ cups dry white wine
1 cup low-salt chicken broth
1 cup canned crushed tomatoes with added puree

Fresh rosemary sprigs

Preheat oven to 325°F. Heat extra-virgin olive oil in heavy large ovenproof pot over medium-high heat. Sprinkle chicken with salt and pepper. Working in 2 batches, sauté chicken until golden, about 4 minutes per side. Transfer chicken to platter. Add prosciutto, sliced garlic, and chopped rosemary to same pot. Stir 1 minute. Add dry white wine, chicken broth, and crushed tomatoes with puree. Bring to boil, scraping up browned bits. Boil 5 minutes. Return chicken to pot, arranging in single layer. Return to boil. Cover pot and

place in oven. Bake until chicken breasts are cooked through, about 20 minutes. Remove chicken breasts. Continue baking until drumsticks and thighs are cooked through, about 10 minutes longer. Remove pot from oven. Return chicken breasts to pot. (*Can be prepared 1 day ahead. Cool slightly. Refrigerate uncovered until cold, then cover and keep refrigerated.*)

Bring chicken mixture to simmer. Transfer chicken to platter; tent with foil. Boil until sauce is reduced to 2 cups and coats back of spoon, about 5 minutes. Season sauce to taste with salt and pepper. Pour sauce over chicken. Garnish with rosemary sprigs and serve.

6 SERVINGS

Chicken Tagine with Chickpeas and Green Beans

- 1 tablespoon olive oil
- 1 large onion, thinly sliced
- 6 large garlic cloves, minced
- 1 tablespoon minced peeled ginger
- 1½ tablespoons paprika
- 1 teaspoon turmeric
- ½ teaspoon ground coriander
- ½ teaspoon ground cumin
- ½ teaspoon cayenne pepper
- ⅛ teaspoon ground cinnamon
- 2 cups (or more) water
- 2 cups drained canned garbanzo beans (chickpeas), from two 15-ounce cans
- ½ cup canned diced tomatoes in juice
- ½ cup chopped fresh cilantro stems
- 1 lemon, quartered, thinly sliced
- 2 tablespoons (or more) fresh lemon juice

- 4 chicken leg-thigh pieces, skin removed, thighs and drumsticks separated
- 2 chicken breast halves with bones, skin removed, each cut crosswise into 2 pieces
- 3 medium carrots, peeled, cut into 2-inch pieces
- 2 cups 2-inch pieces green beans
- ¼ cup chopped fresh mint

Heat oil in heavy large pot over medium heat. Add onion, garlic, and ginger. Cover and cook until onion is tender, stirring often, about 10 minutes. Add paprika and next 5 ingredients; stir 1 minute. Stir in 2 cups water, garbanzo beans, tomatoes with juices, cilantro, lemon, and 2 tablespoons lemon juice. Bring to boil. Reduce heat; cover, and simmer 10 minutes.

Sprinkle chicken with salt and pepper; add to pot. Cover and simmer 30 minutes. Add carrots and more water to cover if liquid has evaporated; cook 10 minutes. Stir in green beans; simmer until chicken and vegetables are tender, about 5 minutes longer. Season with salt and pepper and more lemon juice, if desired. Transfer to bowl. Sprinkle with mint.

4 SERVINGS

Mediterranean Dinner for 4

Spicy Marinated Mozzarella with Oregano and Capers
(page 14)

Chicken Tagine with Chickpeas and Green Beans
(at left; pictured opposite)

Couscous

Gewürztraminer or Syrah

Raisin-Nut Spice Cookies
(page 228)

Coffee

Orange- and Mustard-Basted Turkey with Apple Cider-Mustard Gravy

TURKEY

- 2 tablespoons (¼ stick) butter, room temperature
- 1 tablespoon dried tarragon
- 1 tablespoon dried marjoram
- 1 tablespoon mustard seeds, coarsely crushed
- 2 teaspoons coarse salt
- ½ teaspoon ground black pepper
- 1 12- to 14-pound turkey
- 1 large orange, quartered

- 1 onion, peeled, quartered (optional)
- 1 head of garlic, unpeeled, cut horizontally in half (optional)
- 2 celery stalks, cut into 2-inch lengths (optional)
- 3 fresh thyme sprigs (optional)
- 2 fresh sage sprigs (optional)
- 1 cup orange juice
- 1 tablespoon Dijon mustard
- 5 cups (about) low-salt chicken broth

GRAVY

- 4½ tablespoons butter
- ¾ cup minced onion
- 3 tablespoons all purpose flour
- 1 large Gala apple, peeled, cored, cut into ¼-inch cubes
- 1½ cups whole milk
- 1 cup low-salt chicken broth
- ¾ cup apple cider
- 2 small bay leaves, torn into pieces
- 1 tablespoon Dijon mustard
- 1½ teaspoons mustard seeds, coarsely crushed
- 1½ teaspoons chopped fresh sage

FOR TURKEY: Mix first 6 ingredients in small bowl. Rinse turkey inside and out; pat dry. Place on rack set in large roasting pan. Rub inside of main cavity and neck cavity with orange quarters (reserve orange quarters); sprinkle with salt and pepper. Rub herb butter over outside of turkey. (*Can be prepared 1 day ahead. Cover; chill.*)

Set rack at lowest position in oven and preheat to 350°F. If not stuffing turkey, fill main cavity and neck cavity with orange quarters, onion, garlic, celery, thyme sprigs, and sage sprigs. If stuffing turkey, spoon stuffing loosely into both cavities. Tuck wing tips under; tie legs together loosely to hold shape. Mix orange juice and Dijon mustard in small bowl; pour into pan around turkey. Place turkey in oven with tail at back. Roast turkey 45 minutes. Add 2 cups broth to pan; baste turkey. Turn pan around. Roast turkey 45 minutes. Add 1 cup broth; baste with pan juices. Turn pan around and cover turkey loosely with foil. Continue to roast until thermometer inserted into thickest part of thigh registers 175°F, basting with 1 cup broth and rotating pan every 45 minutes, about 1 hour 45 minutes longer if unstuffed and 2 hours 15 minutes longer if stuffed. Transfer turkey to platter; let stand 30 minutes (internal temperature will increase 5 to 10 degrees).

FOR GRAVY: Strain pan juices into 8-cup measuring cup. Spoon off fat. Melt butter in large saucepan over medium-high heat. Add onion; sauté 3 minutes. Add flour and stir until golden, about 5 minutes. Whisk in apple and all remaining ingredients, then pan juices. Bring gravy to boil. Reduce heat to medium and simmer until gravy thickens, whisking occasionally, about 10 minutes. Season gravy with salt and pepper. Serve turkey with gravy.

8 SERVINGS

Hot Turkey Sandwiches with Sherry Gravy

8 ¼-inch-thick turkey breast scallops (each about 2½ ounces)
3 tablespoons chopped fresh sage or 3 teaspoons dried
¼ cup (½ stick) butter
3 large green onions, thinly sliced
2 tablespoons all purpose flour
1 14½-ounce can low-salt chicken broth
⅓ cup cream Sherry

4 ½-inch-thick diagonal slices sourdough bread (each about 5x3½ inches), lightly toasted, buttered

Sprinkle turkey with half of chopped fresh sage, salt, and pepper. Melt butter in heavy large skillet over medium-high heat. Add 4 turkey scallops and sauté until lightly browned and

cooked through, about 1½ minutes per side. Transfer to plate. Repeat with remaining 4 turkey breast scallops. Add green onions to skillet and sauté 1 minute. Sprinkle with flour; stir 1 minute. Gradually whisk in chicken broth and cream Sherry. Increase heat to high and boil until gravy thickens, whisking constantly, about 2 minutes. Add remaining half of sage. Reduce heat to low. Return turkey and any accumulated juices to gravy; simmer 1 minute to heat through. Season turkey with salt and pepper.

Place 1 bread slice on each plate. Top each with 2 turkey scallops and gravy and serve immediately.

4 SERVINGS

Roast Duck with Lingonberry Sauce

    2 10-ounce jars lingonberries in sugar
    2 teaspoons chopped fresh thyme

    2 5½- to 6-pound ducks (thawed if frozen), rinsed, patted dry, excess
       neck skin cut away
    2 lemons, halved
   10 fresh thyme sprigs

Mix lingonberries and thyme in bowl. (*Can be made 2 days ahead. Cover; chill.*)

Preheat oven to 350°F. Rub outside of each duck with cut side of 1 lemon half; discard lemon halves. Sprinkle duck cavities with salt and pepper. Place 1 lemon half and 5 thyme sprigs into cavity of each duck. Place large rack in large roasting pan. Place ducks on rack. Roast 1½ hours. Remove ducks from oven. Increase oven temperature to 450°F.

Using bulb baster, remove fat from pan. Place wooden spoon in cavity of each duck and tilt duck so juices run into pan; return ducks to rack. Roast until golden brown, about 45 minutes longer. Let ducks stand 10 minutes. Carve ducks; arrange on plates. Serve, passing lingonberry sauce separately.

6 SERVINGS

Roasted Salmon with Corn Relish

2 tablespoons plus 2 teaspoons coriander seeds

RELISH

4 red bell peppers

4 tablespoons extra-virgin olive oil
4 cups fresh corn kernels (from about 4 ears)
4 green onions, thinly sliced
3 garlic cloves, minced
2 tablespoons chopped fresh thyme
1/4 cup dry white wine
2 tablespoons fresh lemon juice
1 tablespoon honey
1/4 cup chopped fresh Italian parsley

SALMON

1/4 cup extra-virgin olive oil
1/4 cup fresh lemon juice
2 tablespoons honey
2 tablespoons paprika
2 teaspoons salt
10 5- to 6-ounce skinless salmon fillets (each about 1¾ inches thick)

Toast coriander seeds in small skillet over medium heat until aromatic, stirring frequently, about 2 minutes. Cool slightly. Crush in mortar with pestle.

FOR RELISH: Char bell peppers over gas flame or under broiler until blackened on all sides. Enclose in paper bag 10 minutes. Peel and seed peppers; cut into 1/2-inch pieces. Set aside.

Heat 2 tablespoons oil in heavy large skillet over medium-high heat. Add corn and green onions and sauté until corn begins to brown in spots, about 5 minutes. Add garlic and thyme; sauté 2 minutes. Add wine and stir until liquid evaporates, about 1 minute. Remove from heat. Stir in bell peppers, lemon juice, honey, and remaining 2 tablespoons olive oil. Add 1½ teaspoons crushed coriander seeds. *(Relish can be made 8 hours ahead. Cover and refrigerate. Stir over medium heat until heated through before serving.)* Stir parsley into relish. Season to taste with salt and pepper.

FOR SALMON: Preheat oven to 400°F. Line large baking sheet with foil. Mix first 5 ingredients and remaining crushed coriander seeds in medium bowl. Brush salmon all over with mixture. Transfer to prepared baking sheet. Roast salmon until opaque in center, about 10 minutes. Transfer to platter. Spoon relish over salmon and serve.

10 SERVINGS

SEAFOOD

Fried Catfish Sandwiches with Curried Mayonnaise

½ cup mayonnaise
1 tablespoon curry powder
1 tablespoon fresh lemon juice
1 18-inch-long French-bread baguette, cut crosswise into 4 equal pieces

½ cup yellow cornmeal
½ cup all purpose flour
½ cup whole milk
4 catfish fillets (each about 5 ounces)
3 tablespoons olive oil

1 large tomato, thinly sliced
4 Boston lettuce leaves

Stir first 3 ingredients in small bowl to blend; season with salt and pepper. Cut bread pieces in half horizontally. Spread bottom halves with curried mayonnaise.

Whisk cornmeal and flour in shallow bowl to blend. Pour milk into another shallow bowl. Dip each fillet into milk, then into cornmeal mixture to coat. Sprinkle with salt and pepper. Heat oil in heavy large skillet over medium-high heat. Add fillets; sauté until cooked through and brown, about 5 minutes per side.

Place fillets on bread bottoms. Top with tomato, lettuce, and bread tops.

4 SERVINGS

Slow-Roasted Tuna with Tomatoes, Herbs, and Spices

1 2¼-pound tuna fillet
9 whole cloves
9 whole coriander seeds
3 large garlic cloves, cut into slivers
⅓ cup extra-virgin olive oil
1 large red onion, thinly sliced
1½ pounds plum tomatoes, halved, seeded, chopped
1 teaspoon dried oregano
⅓ cup white wine vinegar

Preheat oven to 200°F. Using knife, make 9 slits in sides of tuna. Fill each with 1 clove, 1 coriander seed, and 1 garlic sliver; sprinkle tuna with salt and pepper. Heat oil in ovenproof pot over medium heat. Add onion and sauté 8 minutes; push to side of pot. Add tuna and sauté until brown on all sides, about 12 minutes. Scatter tomatoes, oregano, and remaining garlic slivers around tuna. Sprinkle with salt and pepper. Pour vinegar over fish.

Bake tuna uncovered until thermometer inserted into center registers 145°F for medium-rare, about 12 minutes. Transfer tuna to platter. Spoon tomato sauce over. Cool to room temperature. Slice tuna thinly and serve.

6 SERVINGS

Sea Bass with Citrus and Soy

½ cup pineapple juice

½ cup orange juice

⅓ cup soy sauce

3 tablespoons finely chopped peeled fresh ginger

2 tablespoons oriental sesame oil

⅛ teaspoon cayenne pepper

4 6-ounce sea bass fillets

Chopped green onions

Mix first 6 ingredients in 8x8x2-inch glass baking dish. Add fish; turn to coat. Chill 2 hours, turning fish occasionally.

Place steamer rack in large skillet. Arrange fish on rack. Pour marinade into skillet under rack and bring to boil. Cover skillet and steam fish until just opaque in center, about 8 minutes. Transfer fish to plates. Remove steamer rack from skillet. Boil marinade until reduced enough to coat spoon, about 6 minutes; spoon over fish. Top with chopped green onions and serve.

4 SERVINGS

Grilled Whole Fish with Olive Oil and Garlic

7 1¼-pound red snapper or striped bass, scaled, gutted
1½ cups olive oil
3 tablespoons chopped fresh parsley
4 garlic cloves, minced

Lemon wedges

Arrange fish on 2 large rimmed baking sheets. Cut 3 parallel slits in each side of fish, spacing evenly. Mix oil, parsley, and garlic in bowl. Set aside ½ cup oil mixture. Pour remaining mixture over fish; turn to coat. Sprinkle with salt and pepper. Cover; chill at least 1 hour and up to 4 hours.

Prepare grill (medium heat). Lift fish, allowing excess oil to drain off. Grill fish until opaque in center, about 10 minutes per side. Transfer to platter. Pour reserved oil mixture over. Garnish with lemon.

14 SERVINGS

Orange Roughy with Indian-Spiced Tomato Sauce

4 6-ounce orange roughy fillets or red snapper fillets (each about ½ to ¾ inch thick)
3 teaspoons garam masala*
2 tablespoons (¼ stick) butter

1 14½-ounce can diced tomatoes with mild green chilies, undrained
4 tablespoons chopped fresh cilantro
½ cup plain yogurt

Sprinkle fish on both sides with salt and pepper, then with 1 teaspoon garam masala, dividing equally. Melt butter in heavy large skillet over medium heat. Add fish and cook until opaque in center, about 2½ minutes per side. Transfer fish to platter (do not clean skillet).

Add tomatoes with juices, 2 tablespoons cilantro, and remaining 2 teaspoons garam masala to same skillet. Simmer over medium-low heat until slightly thickened, scraping up any browned bits, about 2 minutes. Season with salt and pepper. Spoon sauce over fish. Top with yogurt and sprinkle with remaining 2 tablespoons cilantro.

*A spice mixture available at Indian markets, specialty foods stores, and some supermarkets.

4 SERVINGS

Halibut with Herb Sauce

6 tablespoons fresh lemon juice
6 tablespoons extra-virgin olive oil
3 tablespoons chopped fresh basil
3 tablespoons chopped fresh chives
3 tablespoons chopped fresh parsley

6 6-ounce halibut fillets
2 tablespoons extra-virgin olive oil

Puree first 5 ingredients in processor. Season herb sauce to taste with salt and pepper.

Preheat broiler. Brush fish with 2 tablespoons oil. Sprinkle with salt and pepper. Broil until just opaque in center, about 5 minutes per side. Transfer fish to plates. Spoon sauce over and serve.

6 SERVINGS

Spicy Sautéed Fish with Olives and Cherry Tomatoes

¼ cup olive oil

2 pounds tilapia, red snapper, or orange roughy fillets

½ cup chopped fresh parsley

½ teaspoon dried crushed red pepper

4 cups cherry tomatoes, halved

1 cup Kalamata olives or other brine-cured black olives, chopped

6 garlic cloves, minced

Heat olive oil in heavy large skillet over medium-high heat. Sprinkle fish with salt and pepper. Add half of fish to skillet and sauté until just opaque in center, about 3 minutes per side. Transfer fish to platter. Repeat with remaining fish. Add parsley and crushed red pepper to same skillet; sauté 1 minute. Add tomatoes, olives, and garlic; sauté until tomatoes are soft and juicy, about 2 minutes. Season sauce with salt and pepper; spoon over fish.

4 SERVINGS

Baked Salmon Stuffed with Mascarpone Spinach

1	10-ounce bag fresh spinach leaves
½	cup cream cheese (about 4 ounces), room temperature
½	cup mascarpone cheese,* room temperature
	Pinch of ground nutmeg
8	6- to 8-ounce salmon fillets with skin (each about 1 inch thick)
	Olive oil
2⅔	cups fresh breadcrumbs from French bread with crust
½	cup (1 stick) butter, melted
½	cup freshly grated Parmesan cheese

Cook spinach in large pot of boiling water just until wilted, about 30 seconds. Drain; rinse with cold water. Squeeze spinach dry, then finely chop. Place in small bowl. Mix in cream cheese, mascarpone, and ground nutmeg. Season to taste with salt and pepper. Cut one 3/4-inch-deep, 2 1/2-inch-long slit down center of top side of each salmon fillet, forming pocket for spinach mixture. Fill each slit with spinach mixture, dividing equally among salmon fillets. (*Can be made 4 hours ahead. Cover and chill.*)

Preheat oven to 450°F. Brush rimmed baking sheet with olive oil. Sprinkle salmon fillets with salt and pepper. Mix breadcrumbs, melted butter, and Parmesan cheese in medium bowl. Top each salmon fillet with breadcrumb mixture, pressing to adhere. Place salmon fillets, skin side down, on prepared baking sheet. Bake salmon until opaque in center, about 12 minutes. Transfer to plates and serve.

Italian cream cheese available at Italian markets, specialty foods stores, and also at many supermarkets.

8 SERVINGS

Pacific Coast Bouillabaisse

ROUILLE

- 2 large red bell peppers, coarsely chopped
- 1 cup chopped drained roasted red peppers from jar
- 4 large garlic cloves
- 2 red jalapeño chilies, quartered, with seeds
- 1 cup fresh breadcrumbs made from crustless French bread
- ½ teaspoon salt
- 10 tablespoons olive oil

BOUILLABAISSE

- 6 tablespoons olive oil
- 2 medium leeks (white and pale green parts only), chopped
- 1 medium onion, chopped
- 6 large garlic cloves, chopped
- 3 small bay leaves
- 1½ tablespoons chopped fresh thyme
- ¼ cup chopped fresh parsley
- 1 5x½-inch strip orange peel
- ¼ teaspoon saffron threads, crushed
- 6 (or more) 8-ounce bottles clam juice
- 1 28-ounce can diced tomatoes in juice
- 1¼ cups dry white wine
- ⅔ cup Pernod or other anise-flavored liqueur
- 24 mussels, scrubbed, debearded
- 2 cups water

- 1½ pounds halibut fillets, cut into 1-inch pieces
- 1½ pounds sea bass fillets, cut into 1-inch pieces
- 1½ pounds sea scallops, side muscle removed
- 1½ pounds uncooked shrimp, peeled, deveined

FOR ROUILLE: Combine red bell peppers, roasted peppers, garlic, and chilies in processor. Chop finely, using on/off turns. Add breadcrumbs and salt; blend. Gradually add olive oil, blending until puree forms. Transfer rouille to bowl. Cover and refrigerate. (*Can be prepared 2 days ahead. Keep refrigerated.*)

FOR BOUILLABAISSE: Heat oil in large wide pot over medium-high heat. Add next 5 ingredients; sauté 5 minutes. Add parsley, orange peel, and saffron; stir 30 seconds. Add 6 bottles clam juice, tomatoes with juices, wine, and Pernod. Boil until reduced to medium-thick sauce, stirring often, about 30 minutes. (*Can be made 1 day ahead. Chill uncovered.*)

Combine mussels and 2 cups water in large pot over high heat. Bring to boil; cover and

cook until mussels open, about 5 minutes. Transfer mussels to bowl (discard any mussels that do not open).

Strain mussel broth into bouillabaisse; bring to simmer, stirring often. Add fish, scallops, and shrimp. Simmer until fish and shellfish are just opaque in center, gently stirring occasionally and adding mussels during last 3 minutes, about 8 minutes. Add more clam juice if thinner broth is desired. Ladle bouillabaisse into large shallow bowls. Serve, passing rouille separately.

10 SERVINGS

Scallops with Mashed Potatoes and Tarragon Sauce

  2   pounds Yukon Gold potatoes, peeled, cut into 1-inch pieces
  1   teaspoon salt
  ½   cup (1 stick) plus 1 tablespoon butter, room temperature
  ⅔   cup (or more) whole milk

  12 sea scallops, side muscles trimmed

  ⅓   cup dry white wine
  2   tablespoons chopped shallot
  2   tablespoons whipping cream
  1½ tablespoons plus ¼ cup chopped fresh tarragon

Place potatoes in large pot. Cover with cold water. Add 1 teaspoon salt and bring to boil over high heat. Boil until potatoes are tender when pierced with skewer, about 8 minutes. Drain. Return to pot. Using potato masher, mash potatoes. Mash in ¼ cup butter. Stir in ⅔ cup milk. Season to taste with salt and pepper. (*Can be made 1 hour ahead. Let stand at room temperature. Before serving, stir over medium heat until heated through, adding more milk by tablespoonfuls if dry.*)

Melt 1 tablespoon butter in large skillet over medium-high heat. Sprinkle scallops with salt and pepper. Add scallops to skillet; sauté until just opaque in center, about 2 minutes per side. Transfer to plate; tent with foil. Reserve juices in skillet.

Place wine and shallots in small saucepan. Simmer over medium heat until reduced to glaze, about 3 minutes. Stir in cream; simmer 1 minute. Gradually whisk in remaining ¼ cup butter. Stir in reserved pan juices. Stir in 1½ tablespoons tarragon. Season tarragon sauce to taste with salt and pepper.

Stir remaining ¼ cup tarragon into warm mashed potatoes. Divide potatoes among 4 shallow bowls. Place scallops atop mashed potatoes. Drizzle with tarragon sauce and serve.

4 SERVINGS

Elegant Dinner for 4

Champagne

Caviar with Toast Points

Scallops with Mashed Potatoes and Tarragon Sauce
(*at left; pictured opposite*)

Green Beans with Citrus Butter Sauce
(*page 143*)

Sauvignon Blanc

Phyllo Cups with Chocolate Mousse and Fresh Fruit
(*page 206*)

Chili-Glazed Shrimp with Tomatillo-Cilantro Sauce

1 pound tomatillos,* husked

1 onion, coarsely chopped

1 tablespoon minced seeded jalapeño chili

1 garlic clove, crushed

3 tablespoons extra-virgin olive oil

2 tablespoons chopped cilantro

24 jumbo shrimp, peeled, deveined, tails left intact

2 tablespoons ground mild chili (such as ancho or New Mexican*)

1 teaspoon onion powder

½ teaspoon garlic powder

Queso fresco* or feta cheese

Cook tomatillos in large pot of boiling salted water until olive-green color, about 5 minutes. Drain and transfer to blender. Add onion, jalapeño, and garlic and process tomatillo sauce until smooth.

Heat 1 tablespoon oil in skillet over medium heat. Add sauce and bring to boil. Reduce heat and simmer until slightly thickened, stirring occasionally, about 5 minutes. Stir in cilantro. Season with salt and pepper. Cool to room temperature. (*Can be made 1 day ahead. Chill. Bring to room temperature before using.*)

Prepare barbecue (medium-high heat). Toss shrimp with remaining 2 tablespoons oil in large bowl. Add ground chili, onion powder, and garlic powder; toss to combine. Sprinkle shrimp with salt and pepper. Grill shrimp until just cooked through, about 2 minutes per side.

Spoon about 3 tablespoons tomatillo sauce into center of each of 6 plates. Arrange shrimp atop sauce. Sprinkle with queso fresco.

Tomatillos (green tomato-like vegetables with paper-thin husks), ground New Mexican chilies, and queso fresco (also known as queso blanco) are sold at Latin American markets and some supermarkets.

6 SERVINGS

Pesto-Tomato Clams

1 cup dry white wine

3 garlic cloves, minced

½ teaspoon dried crushed red pepper

8 pounds littleneck clams, scrubbed

3 cups chopped plum tomatoes

1 7- to 8-ounce container purchased basil pesto

Bring wine, garlic, and crushed red pepper to boil in heavy extra-large pot. Add clams. Cover and cook until clams open, about 9 minutes. Using slotted spoon or tongs, transfer clams to 4 large bowls (discard any clams that do not open). Stir tomatoes and pesto into pot and bring to simmer. Ladle pesto broth over clams and serve.

4 SERVINGS

Baked Shrimp with Feta and Olives

⅓ cup plus 3 tablespoons olive oil
3 medium onions, chopped
2 14½-ounce cans peeled diced tomatoes in juice
4 tablespoons chopped fresh parsley
1 tablespoon dried oregano
5 garlic cloves, minced
½ teaspoon cayenne pepper

2 pounds uncooked large shrimp, peeled, deveined (tails left intact)
½ cup ouzo (unsweetened anise liqueur)
½ cup Kalamata olives or other brine-cured olives pitted, halved
8 ounces feta cheese, crumbled
Toasted French-bread slices

Heat ⅓ cup oil in large saucepan over medium heat. Add onions; sauté until golden, about 12 minutes. Add tomatoes with juices, 3 tablespoons parsley, oregano, garlic, and cayenne. Bring to boil. Reduce heat to medium-low. Cover; simmer until sauce thickens, about 20 minutes. Season sauce with salt and pepper. Transfer to medium bowl. *(Can be made 1 day ahead. Cover; chill. Rewarm before continuing.)*

Preheat oven to 400°F. Heat 3 tablespoons oil in heavy large skillet over medium-high heat. Sprinkle shrimp with salt and pepper. Add to skillet; sauté until almost opaque in center, about 3 minutes. Remove skillet from heat. Add ouzo. Carefully ignite ouzo with match. Return skillet to medium heat; cook shrimp until flames subside. Add tomato sauce and olives; stir. Transfer shrimp mixture to 10- to 12-cup baking dish. Sprinkle cheese over. Bake until shrimp are cooked through, about 10 minutes. Sprinkle with 1 tablespoon parsley. Serve immediately with toasts.

8 SERVINGS

Artichoke and Mushroom Lasagna

FILLING

- 2 tablespoons (¼ stick) butter
- 1 pound mushrooms, sliced
- 3 garlic cloves, minced
- 2 8-ounce packages frozen artichoke hearts, thawed, coarsely chopped
- 1 cup dry vermouth

BÉCHAMEL SAUCE

- 4½ tablespoons butter
- 4½ tablespoons all purpose flour
- 4½ cups whole milk
- 2½ cups freshly grated Parmesan cheese (about 7½ ounces)
  Ground nutmeg

- 1 9-ounce package oven-ready (no-boil) lasagna noodles
- 1 pound whole-milk mozzarella cheese, thinly sliced

FOR FILLING: Melt butter in large skillet over medium-high heat. Add mushrooms and garlic; sauté until mushrooms begin to brown, about 7 minutes. Add artichokes and vermouth. Cook until liquid is absorbed, stirring occasionally, 10 minutes. Season with salt and pepper.

FOR BÉCHAMEL SAUCE: Melt butter in heavy medium saucepan over medium-high heat. Add flour; stir 1 minute. Gradually whisk in milk. Reduce heat to medium and simmer until sauce thickens and lightly coats spoon, stirring occasionally, about 20 minutes. Stir in 1½ cups Parmesan. Season to taste with salt, pepper, and ground nutmeg.

Spread ⅔ cup béchamel sauce over bottom of 13x9x2-inch glass baking dish. Top with enough noodles to cover bottom of dish. Spread ¼ of artichoke mixture over. Spoon ⅔ cup béchamel sauce over. Top béchamel with ¼ of mozzarella. Sprinkle with 3 tablespoons Parmesan. Top with enough noodles to cover. Repeat layering 3 more times, finishing with a layer of noodles, then remaining béchamel. Top with remaining Parmesan. (*Can be made 1 day ahead. Cover with foil; chill.*)

Preheat oven to 350°F. Bake lasagna covered with foil 1 hour (or 1 hour 15 minutes if chilled). Remove foil. Increase temperature to 450°F. Bake lasagna until golden on top, about 10 minutes longer.

8 SERVINGS

Herbed Cheese Scrambled Eggs on Asparagus

1	pound slender asparagus spears, trimmed
½	cup creamy garlic and herb cheese (such as Boursin)
1	tablespoon minced fresh basil
10	large eggs
2½	tablespoons butter

Cook asparagus in medium skillet of boiling water until just tender, about 3 minutes. Drain; return asparagus to skillet. Mix cheese and basil in small bowl. Whisk eggs in large bowl. Melt 1½ tablespoons butter in heavy large skillet over medium heat. Add eggs; stir until eggs are almost set, about 1 minute. Add cheese mixture and stir until cheese melts and eggs are softly set, about 2 minutes.

Meanwhile, add 1 tablespoon butter to asparagus in skillet and stir over medium heat. Divide asparagus among 4 plates; spoon eggs over and serve.

4 SERVINGS

Spring Vegetable Paella

    2 large fresh fennel bulbs (about 1½ pounds total), trimmed, each cut into 8 wedges;
        2 tablespoons chopped fronds reserved
   12 ounces baby carrots (from about 4 bunches), trimmed, peeled
    8 ounces turnips, peeled, cut into ¾-inch pieces (about 1½ cups)
    8 ounces 1½-inch red-skinned new potatoes, halved
   ¼ cup plus 3 tablespoons olive oil

   ¼ cup plus 1 tablespoon chopped fresh parsley
    4 garlic cloves, chopped
    1 tablespoon paprika
    1 teaspoon saffron threads, crushed
    1 teaspoon salt

    1 onion, chopped
    4 plum tomatoes, chopped, seeds and juices reserved
   2¼ cups arborio rice or medium-grain rice
    1 14-ounce can vegetable broth
    2 cups water
   ¾ cup dry white wine
    1 pound asparagus, trimmed, cut into 1-inch pieces
    1 cup drained canned garbanzo beans (chickpeas)

Preheat oven to 450°F. Toss fennel bulbs, carrots, turnips, potatoes, and ¼ cup oil in large bowl. Sprinkle generously with salt and pepper. Transfer to large rimmed baking sheet. Roast until tender and brown around edges, about 1 hour.

Finely mince ¼ cup parsley and garlic together. Transfer to small bowl. Stir in paprika, saffron, and 1 teaspoon salt.

Heat remaining 3 tablespoons oil in large skillet over medium-high heat. Add onion and sauté until soft, about 8 minutes. Add tomatoes; sauté 2 minutes. Add rice and parsley mixture; stir 2 minutes. Stir in broth, water, and wine; bring to boil. Reduce heat to low, cover, and simmer 15 minutes. Stir in asparagus, garbanzo beans, and roasted vegetables. Increase heat to medium-low; cover and simmer until liquid is absorbed, stirring often, about 20 minutes. Season paella with salt and pepper. Transfer to large platter. Sprinkle with reserved fennel fronds and remaining parsley.

6 SERVINGS

Portobellos Stuffed with Corn and Mushrooms

  1 cup plus 3 tablespoons corn oil
10 garlic cloves, minced
  2 tablespoons white balsamic vinegar
  5 teaspoons chopped fresh thyme
  4 teaspoons chopped fresh oregano

  8 5-inch-diameter portobello mushrooms

  1 pound assorted fresh wild mushrooms (such as oyster and stemmed shiitake), sliced
1½ cups fresh corn kernels
¾ cup whipping cream
  1 cup crumbled Cotija or feta cheese

Whisk 1 cup oil, garlic, vinegar, 3 teaspoons thyme, and 2 teaspoons oregano in medium bowl to blend. Season generously with salt and pepper. Transfer 1/3 cup garlic-herb oil to small bowl; reserve.

Trim and thinly slice portobello stems; set aside. Brush both sides of portobello caps with remaining garlic-herb oil; place caps, rounded side down, on large rimmed baking sheet.

Preheat broiler. Broil portobello caps until tender, about 5 minutes per side. Remove from broiler. Turn caps rounded side down. Heat 3 tablespoons oil in heavy large skillet over medium-high heat. Add assorted mushrooms and portobello stems; sauté 5 minutes. Stir in reserved 1/3 cup garlic-herb oil; sauté until mushrooms are tender, about 5 minutes. Add corn; sauté until tender, about 3 minutes. Add cream; simmer until almost absorbed, about 2 minutes. Stir in cheese. Season with salt and pepper. Divide mixture among portobello caps, mounding in center. (*Can be made 6 hours ahead. Cover; chill.*)

Preheat broiler. Broil portobellos until heated through, about 5 minutes. Sprinkle with 2 teaspoons each thyme and oregano.

8 SERVINGS

Tomato, Black-Eyed Pea, and Bell Pepper Stew

  ¼ cup olive oil
  3 cups chopped bell peppers (mix of yellow, orange, and green)
  1 onion, chopped
  4 teaspoons ancho chili powder or other chili powder
  2 14½-ounce cans fire-roasted tomatoes in juice
  1 1-pound package frozen black-eyed peas
2½ cups canned vegetable broth

1½ cups shredded Mexican four-cheese mix

Heat oil in heavy large pot over medium-high heat. Add bell peppers and onion; sauté until soft, about 5 minutes. Stir in chili powder; sauté 1 minute. Stir in tomatoes with juices, black-eyed peas, and broth. Bring to simmer. Reduce heat to medium-low; partially cover and simmer until peas are tender, about 35 minutes. Season stew to taste with salt and pepper. (*Can be made 1 day ahead. Cool slightly. Chill uncovered until cold, then cover and chill. Bring to simmer before serving.*)

Divide stew among 6 bowls. Top each with ¼ cup cheese and serve.

6 SERVINGS

Curried Couscous with Roasted Vegetables, Peach Chutney, and Cilantro Yogurt

CILANTRO YOGURT

- 3 cups (loosely packed) fresh cilantro leaves (from 3 large bunches)
- 1 tablespoon fresh lime juice
- ¾ teaspoon salt
- ½ cup plain whole-milk yogurt
- ½ cup sour cream

ROASTED VEGETABLES

- Nonstick vegetable oil spray
- 2 1-pound eggplants, unpeeled, cut into 1-inch cubes
- 6 tablespoons corn oil
- 1¼ pounds medium zucchini, halved lengthwise, cut crosswise into 1-inch pieces
- 3 large red bell peppers

COUSCOUS

- 2 tablespoons corn oil
- 1 medium onion, chopped
- 1 tablespoon curry powder
- 3 cups water
- 2 cups (12 ounces) plain couscous
- ½ cup coarsely chopped roasted salted cashews
- ¼ cup dried currants
- Peach Chutney (see recipe on next page)

FOR YOGURT: Combine cilantro, lime juice, and salt in processor; blend to coarse puree. Transfer to medium bowl; mix in yogurt and sour cream. Season with pepper. (*Can be made 1 day ahead. Cover and chill.*)

FOR VEGETABLES: Preheat oven to 400°F. Spray 2 large baking sheets with nonstick spray. Mound eggplant cubes on 1 sheet; drizzle with 4 tablespoons oil. Sprinkle with salt and pepper; toss to coat. Spread out evenly. Mound zucchini on second sheet; drizzle with remaining 2 tablespoons oil. Sprinkle with salt and pepper; toss to coat. Spread out evenly. Roast eggplant and zucchini until golden and tender, turning occasionally with spatula, about 25 minutes for zucchini and 50 minutes for eggplant. Transfer vegetables to bowl and cool.

Meanwhile, char peppers directly over gas flame or in broiler until blackened on all sides. Enclose in paper bag; let stand 10 minutes. Peel and seed peppers. Cut 2 peppers into 1-inch pieces. Thinly slice remaining pepper and reserve for garnish.

FOR COUSCOUS: Heat 1 tablespoon oil in heavy large saucepan over medium-high heat. Add onion; sauté until soft, about 6 minutes. Mix in curry powder; stir 1 minute. Add 3 cups water; bring to simmer. Cover; reduce heat to medium-low and simmer curry water 10 minutes.

Heat remaining 1 tablespoon oil in heavy large pot. Add couscous and stir constantly until color darkens and couscous is toasted, about 3 minutes. Mix in hot curry water. Turn off heat, cover pot, and let stand until couscous is tender and curry water is absorbed, about 10 minutes. Fluff couscous with fork to separate grains. Mix in cashews and currants and cool completely. Mix in eggplant, zucchini, and bell pepper pieces. Season to taste with salt and pepper.

Mound on large platter; garnish with reserved bell pepper slices. Serve with cilantro yogurt and chutney.

6 TO 8 SERVINGS

Peach Chutney

- 4 green onions, chopped
- ¼ cup dried currants
- 1 tablespoon Sherry wine vinegar
- 2 teaspoons grated peeled fresh ginger
- 1¾ pounds peaches (about 4 medium), peeled, halved, pitted

Combine onions, currants, vinegar, and ginger in medium bowl. Cut peaches into ⅓-inch cubes. Add to onion mixture and toss to coat. Cover; chill at least 1 hour and up to 6 hours, tossing occasionally.

MAKES ABOUT 4 CUPS

Herbed Goat Cheese and Roasted-Vegetable Sandwiches

Nonstick vegetable oil spray
2 medium zucchini, each cut lengthwise into 4 slices
1 large red bell pepper, quartered
1 large eggplant, cut crosswise into ½-inch-thick slices
2 tablespoons extra-virgin olive oil

3 teaspoons chopped fresh oregano
3 teaspoons chopped fresh thyme
1 tablespoon red wine vinegar

⅔ cup soft fresh goat cheese, room temperature (about 5 ounces)
1 teaspoon grated lemon peel
8 slices whole grain bread or whole grain rolls
2 cups (packed) baby spinach leaves

Preheat oven to 400°F. Spray 2 large baking sheets with nonstick spray. Arrange zucchini, bell pepper, and eggplant on prepared baking sheets. Drizzle with 1 tablespoon oil. Sprinkle with salt and pepper. Roast 15 minutes. Turn vegetables over. Roast until tender and brown in spots, about 10 minutes longer for zucchini and 25 minutes longer for bell pepper and eggplant.

Whisk 1½ teaspoons oregano, 1½ teaspoons thyme, vinegar, and remaining 1 tablespoon oil in large bowl to blend. Add roasted vegetables and toss to coat.

Mix cheese, 1½ teaspoons oregano, 1½ teaspoons thyme, and lemon peel in medium bowl. Place all bread slices on work surface. Spread each with cheese mixture. Top 4 bread slices with roasted vegetables, then spinach leaves. Cover with remaining bread slices, cheese side down. Cut each sandwich in half.

4 SERVINGS

Blueberry Pancakes

1 cup plus 2 tablespoons cake flour
1 cup all purpose flour
¼ cup sugar
1 tablespoon baking powder
½ teaspoon salt
2 cups whole milk
2 large eggs
3 tablespoons unsalted butter, melted, plus additional melted butter

2 ½-pint baskets blueberries
Maple syrup

Whisk first 5 ingredients in large bowl. Whisk milk and eggs in medium bowl. Gradually whisk milk mixture into dry ingredients. Mix in 3 tablespoons melted butter.

Heat griddle or 2 heavy large nonstick skillets over medium heat. Brush lightly with additional melted butter. Working in batches, pour batter by ¼ cupfuls onto griddle. Sprinkle each pancake with 1 heaping tablespoon blueberries. Cook until bottoms brown, about 1½ minutes. Turn pancakes over and cook until second sides brown, about 1 minute. Divide pancakes among plates. Serve with syrup.

4 SERVINGS

Savory Bread Pudding with Gruyère and Fines Herbes

1	1-pound loaf French bread, cut into 1½-inch pieces
1	pound asparagus, trimmed, cut into 1½-inch lengths
6	large eggs
2	cups whole milk
2	teaspoons salt
1	teaspoon ground black pepper
2	cups grated Gruyère cheese
2	cups grated Swiss cheese
1	cup grated Parmesan cheese
⅓	cup chopped fresh chives
⅓	cup chopped fresh parsley
⅓	cup chopped fresh marjoram

Place bread on 2 large baking sheets. Let stand overnight to dry out.

Cook asparagus in medium pot of boiling salted water until crisp-tender, about 3 minutes. Drain. Rinse under cold water to cool. Drain.

Whisk eggs, milk, salt, and pepper in large bowl. Mix cheeses and herbs in medium bowl. Place half of bread in 13x9x2-inch glass baking dish. Sprinkle with half of asparagus, then half of cheese mixture. Pour half of egg mixture over. Repeat with remaining bread, asparagus, cheese mixture, and egg mixture. Let stand 20 minutes, pressing with spatula to submerge bread pieces.

Preheat oven to 375°F. Bake bread pudding until brown and puffed, about 45 minutes. Cool bread pudding 10 minutes and serve.

4 TO 6 SERVINGS

Picnic Lunch for 4

Whole Wheat Pita Chips with Garbanzo Bean-Cumin Dip
(page 12)

Herbed Goat Cheese and Roasted-Vegetable Sandwiches
(opposite)

Fresh Fruit

Beaujolais

Raspberry-Pecan Blondies
(page 231)

Spicy Tofu Satay and Peanut Sauce

2 12-ounce blocks extra-firm tofu, each cut crosswise into 4 slices then horizontally in half, forming sixteen 3½ x 1¼ x ½-inch pieces

16 8-inch wooden skewers

MARINADE

¼ cup vegetable broth

¼ cup unsweetened light coconut milk*

1½ tablespoons mild curry paste*

1 teaspoon minced peeled fresh ginger

1 teaspoon ground turmeric

SATAY SAUCE

½ cup hot water

½ cup chunky peanut butter

¼ cup unsweetened light coconut milk

2 tablespoons honey

2 tablespoons tamari soy sauce*

1 tablespoon tamarind concentrate**

1 tablespoon fresh lime juice

Nonstick vegetable oil spray

Thread 1 tofu piece length-wise on each of 16 skewers. Place tofu skewers on paper towels to drain 1 hour.

FOR MARINADE: Whisk all ingredients in small bowl to blend. Arrange all tofu skewers in 13x9x2-inch glass baking dish. Pour marinade over; lift skewers briefly to allow some marinade to flow underneath. Let stand 2 hours or cover and refrigerate up to 1 day.

FOR SATAY SAUCE: Blend first 7 ingredients in blender until smooth. Season sauce with salt and pepper.

Spray grill rack with non-stick spray. Prepare barbecue

(medium-high heat). Grill tofu skewers until heated through, about 2 minutes per side. Transfer skewers to plates. Serve with satay sauce.

*Unsweetened light coconut milk, mild curry paste, and tamari soy sauce are available at Asian markets and in the Asian section of many supermarkets.
**Tamarind concentrate, a tart, seedless paste, is available at Middle Eastern, Indian, and some Asian markets.

4 SERVINGS

Baked Polenta with Swiss Chard and Cheese

2	tablespoons extra-virgin olive oil
1	large white onion, thinly sliced
2	garlic cloves, minced
¼	teaspoon dried crushed red pepper
1	pound Swiss chard, thick stems and ribs removed, leaves cut crosswise into ½-inch-wide strips

3½	cups water
1	teaspoon salt
1	cup polenta (coarse cornmeal) or yellow cornmeal

1	cup part-skim ricotta cheese
2	large eggs
2	cups coarsely grated low-fat mozzarella cheese (about 8 ounces)

Preheat oven to 350°F. Lightly oil 2-quart glass baking dish. Heat oil in heavy large deep skillet over medium heat. Add onion; sauté until tender, about 15 minutes. Stir in garlic and crushed red pepper, then chard; cover and cook until chard is tender, stirring occasionally, about 8 minutes. Uncover; stir until any excess liquid in skillet evaporates. Season with salt and pepper.

Meanwhile, bring 3½ cups water and salt to boil in heavy large saucepan. Gradually stir polenta into boiling water. Reduce heat to medium-low; simmer until polenta is very thick, stirring frequently, about 10 minutes. Remove from heat.

Whisk ricotta and eggs in bowl; whisk in 1 cup hot polenta. Stir ricotta mixture into polenta in saucepan. Spread half of polenta mixture in baking dish. Spread half of chard mixture over. Sprinkle with half of mozzarella. Repeat layering with remaining polenta, chard, and cheese. Bake until puffed and brown on top, about 45 minutes. Cool 30 minutes.

8 SERVINGS

Potato and Cheese Ravioli with Fresh Tomato Sauce

1¼ pounds russet potatoes, peeled, quartered
1¼ cups freshly grated pecorino Sardo or pecorino Romano cheese
2 tablespoons chopped fresh mint

    All purpose flour
1 12-ounce package wonton wrappers

2 tablespoons extra-virgin olive oil
1 large garlic clove, minced
2 pounds tomatoes, chopped

Cook potatoes in large saucepan of boiling salted water until very tender, about 20 minutes. Drain. Return potatoes to pan and mash. Cool potatoes. Stir in 1 cup cheese and mint. Season filling to taste with salt and pepper.

Line 2 baking sheets with plastic wrap; sprinkle with flour. Stack 6 wonton wrappers on work surface. Trim edges of wonton stack to form 2¾-inch square, preferably using scallop-edged pastry wheel cutter. Repeat stacking and trimming with remaining wrappers. Place half of wrappers on work surface. Place 1 tablespoon filling in center of each. Brush edges of wrappers lightly with water. Top each with another wrapper; press on edges to seal well. Place ravioli on prepared baking sheets. *(Can be made 4 hours ahead. Sprinkle lightly with flour. Cover with plastic wrap and chill.)*

Heat oil in large nonstick skillet over medium heat. Add garlic and stir 30 seconds. Add tomatoes and sauté until heated through, about 5 minutes. Season sauce to taste with salt and pepper. Transfer 1/2 cup sauce to large shallow serving bowl.

Working in batches, cook ravioli in large pot of boiling salted water until just tender but still firm to bite, about 3 minutes. Using slotted spoon, transfer ravioli to bowl with sauce. Spoon remaining sauce over. Sprinkle with remaining 1/4 cup cheese and serve.

2 TO 4 SERVINGS

Linguine with Chipotle and Red Pepper Sauce

3	tablespoons olive oil
1½	large red onions, thinly sliced
2	red bell peppers, thinly sliced
1/3	cup dry Sherry
1	12-ounce jar roasted red peppers, drained, thinly sliced
2	garlic cloves, minced
2	teaspoons minced canned chipotle chilies*
1	pound linguine
1/4	cup chopped fresh parsley
2	tablespoons balsamic vinegar
1	cup freshly grated Manchego cheese

Heat olive oil in large nonstick skillet over high heat. Add red onions and red bell peppers; sauté until onions are brown, about 15 minutes. Stir in Sherry, roasted red peppers, garlic, and chipotles. Simmer until liquid evaporates, about 6 minutes.

Cook linguine in large pot of boiling salted water until tender but still firm to bite, stirring occasionally. Drain linguine, reserving 1/4 cup cooking liquid. Return linguine to pot. Add pepper mixture, parsley, vinegar, and reserved 1/4 cup cooking liquid; toss well. Season to taste with salt and pepper. Divide among bowls. Top with Manchego cheese.

Chipotle chilies canned in a spicy tomato sauce, sometimes called adobo, *are available at Latin American markets and some supermarkets.*

4 SERVINGS

Latin Dinner for 4

Apricot, Berry, and Jicama Salad
with Honey-Lime Dressing
(page 149)

Linguine with Chipotle and
Red Pepper Sauce
(at left)

Mexican Beer

Flans with Marsala and
Caramel Sauce
(page 214)

Spaghetti with Fresh Clams, Parsley, and Lemon

½ cup extra-virgin olive oil

8 garlic cloves, thinly sliced

3 pounds fresh Manila clams or small littleneck clams, scrubbed

¼ cup plus 2 tablespoons chopped fresh Italian parsley

½ cup dry white wine

¼ cup fresh lemon juice

1 pound spaghetti

Heat oil in heavy large pot over medium-high heat. Add sliced garlic and sauté until light brown, about 1 minute. Add clams and ¼ cup chopped Italian parsley; stir 2 minutes. Add wine; simmer 2 minutes. Add fresh lemon juice. Cover and simmer until clams open, about 6 minutes (discard any clams that do not open).

Meanwhile, cook pasta in pot of boiling salted water until just tender but still firm to bite. Drain. Add to clams; toss to coat. Season with salt and pepper. Sprinkle with 2 tablespoons parsley and serve.

4 SERVINGS

Ditalini with Pesto, Beans, and Broccoli Rabe

8 ounces ditalini or other short tube-shaped pasta (about 2 cups)

1 pound broccoli rabe, cut into 2-inch pieces

1 14-ounce can vegetable broth

½ teaspoon dried crushed red pepper

1 15-ounce can cannellini (white kidney beans), rinsed, drained

1 7-ounce container purchased pesto

1 tablespoon white wine vinegar

Cook pasta in large pot of boiling salted water 3 minutes. Add broccoli rabe and boil until broccoli rabe is just crisp-tender and pasta is just tender but still firm to bite, stirring occasionally, about 5 minutes longer. Drain pasta and broccoli rabe, reserving ½ cup cooking liquid. Return pasta and broccoli rabe to pot.

Meanwhile, bring vegetable broth and crushed red pepper to simmer in medium saucepan. Add beans and simmer until heated through, stirring often, about 5 minutes.

Add bean mixture, pesto, and vinegar to pasta and broccoli rabe. Stir well, adding pasta cooking liquid by tablespoonfuls if necessary. Season with salt and pepper and serve.

4 SERVINGS

Fusilli with Eggplant, Pine Nuts, Currants, and Capers

2 16-ounce eggplants, cut crosswise into ½-inch-thick slices

2 tablespoons olive oil
1 medium onion, chopped
4 garlic cloves, minced
¾ cup pine nuts, toasted
¾ cup dried currants
½ cup drained capers
2 14½-ounce cans diced tomatoes in juice

1 pound fusilli pasta
1 cup freshly grated pecorino Romano cheese
½ cup chopped fresh basil

Place eggplant slices on large rimmed baking sheet. Sprinkle with salt. Let stand 20 minutes. Turn eggplant slices over. Sprinkle with salt. Let stand 20 minutes longer. Rinse eggplant.

Drain; pat dry with paper towels. Cut into $1/2$-inch cubes. Set aside.

Heat olive oil in heavy large skillet over medium-high heat. Add onion and sauté until golden, about 4 minutes. Add garlic; sauté 1 minute. Add eggplant; sauté until tender, about 10 minutes. Stir in pine nuts, currants, and capers; sauté 1 minute. Add tomatoes with juices; bring to simmer. Season to taste with salt and pepper.

Meanwhile, cook pasta in large pot of boiling salted water until just tender but still firm to bite. Drain. Return pasta to pot. Add eggplant mixture, $1/4$ cup cheese, and basil. Toss to combine. Transfer to large bowl. Serve, passing remaining cheese separately.

6 SERVINGS

Pasta Shells with Chicken, Escarole, and Sun-Dried Tomatoes

2 tablespoons extra-virgin olive oil
1 cup sliced stemmed fresh shiitake mushrooms (about 2 ounces)
2 garlic cloves, minced
$1/8$ teaspoon dried crushed red pepper
2 cups low-salt chicken broth
8 cups coarsely chopped trimmed escarole (about 1 large bunch)

2 cups medium pasta shells (about 5 ounces)
2 cups $3/4$-inch pieces skinless roasted chicken
$1/4$ cup thinly sliced drained oil-packed sun-dried tomatoes
$1/4$ cup grated Parmesan cheese

Heat oil in large deep nonstick skillet over medium heat. Add mushrooms and sauté until tender, about 4 minutes. Add garlic and red pepper and stir 1 minute. Add broth and bring to boil. Stir in escarole; cover and cook 5 minutes. Uncover; cook until escarole is tender, stirring often, about 3 minutes longer. Season with salt and pepper.

Meanwhile, cook pasta in large pot of boiling salted water until just tender but still firm to bite. Drain; return to pot. Add escarole mixture, chicken, and sun-dried tomatoes. Stir over medium heat until chicken is heated through, about 3 minutes. Season with salt and pepper. Transfer to bowl; sprinkle with cheese.

4 SERVINGS

Farfalle with Forest Mushrooms, Peas, and Parsley

¼ cup (½ stick) butter

4 large garlic cloves, minced

3 shallots, chopped

12 ounces shiitake mushrooms, stemmed, quartered

12 ounces crimini mushrooms, quartered

12 ounces chanterelle or crimini mushrooms, quartered

1¼ cups dry white wine

1½ cups whipping cream

2 cups frozen peas

⅔ cup chopped fresh parsley

1¼ pounds farfalle (bow-tie pasta)

Melt butter in large deep skillet over medium-high heat. Add garlic and shallots; sauté 1 minute. Add shiitake and crimini mushrooms and sauté 5 minutes. Add chanterelles; sauté until all mushrooms are tender, about 5 minutes longer. Add wine and boil until reduced by half, about 5 minutes. Add cream and simmer until liquid is reduced to sauce consistency, stirring occasionally, about 5 minutes. Stir in peas and parsley. Remove from heat. Season sauce with salt and pepper. Cover to keep warm.

Meanwhile, cook pasta in large pot of boiling salted water until just tender but still firm to bite, stirring occasionally. Drain, reserving 1 cup pasta cooking liquid. Return pasta to pot.

Add mushroom sauce to pasta and toss to coat, moistening with reserved pasta cooking liquid, if necessary.

6 SERVINGS

Greek-Style Penne with Fresh Tomatoes, Feta, and Dill

2 pounds tomatoes, halved, seeded, chopped

1 cup chopped green onions (white and pale green parts only)

7 ounces feta cheese, crumbled

6 tablespoons chopped fresh parsley

¼ cup chopped fresh dill

¼ cup extra-virgin olive oil

12 ounces penne pasta

Mix first 6 ingredients in large bowl. Set tomato mixture aside.

Cook pasta in large pot of boiling salted water until just tender but still firm to bite, stirring occasionally. Drain. Add hot pasta to tomato mixture and toss to coat. Season to taste with salt and pepper and serve.

4 TO 6 SERVINGS

Penne with Roasted-Tomato Sauce, Orange, and Olives

Nonstick vegetable oil spray
2 pounds plum tomatoes, each cut into 6 wedges
1 onion, halved lengthwise, cut into thin wedges
2 tablespoons extra-virgin olive oil
4 garlic cloves, coarsely chopped
1 tablespoon grated orange peel
½ cup orange juice

2 cups penne (about 8 ounces)
¾ cup chopped fresh basil
¼ cup chopped pitted Kalamata olives or other brine-cured olives
¼ cup freshly grated pecorino Romano cheese

Position 1 rack in bottom third of oven and 1 rack in middle of oven; preheat to 450°F. Spray 2 rimmed baking sheets with nonstick spray. Spread tomatoes on 1 sheet and onion on second sheet. Drizzle 1 tablespoon oil over vegetables on each. Sprinkle garlic and orange peel over both. Sprinkle with salt and pepper. Roast until vegetables are very tender and brown around edges, stirring occasionally, about 30 minutes for onion and 45 minutes for tomatoes. Cool slightly. Pour ¼ cup orange juice over vegetables on each sheet, scraping up any browned bits from bottom of sheets.

Meanwhile, cook pasta in large pot of boiling salted water until just tender but still firm to bite. Reserve ½ cup pasta cooking water. Drain pasta; return to pot. Add tomato and onion mixtures, basil, and olives to pasta. Stir over medium heat until heated through, adding enough reserved pasta cooking water to moisten. Transfer to bowl. Sprinkle with cheese.

4 SERVINGS

Bucatini Carbonara with Zucchini

  6 ounces sliced pancetta or bacon, cut into ¼-inch-wide strips
½ cup whipping cream
  1 garlic clove, finely chopped
¼ teaspoon dried crushed red pepper

  2 tablespoons olive oil
1½ pounds zucchini, thinly sliced

  1 pound bucatini or spaghetti

  3 large eggs
  1 cup freshly grated Parmesan cheese

Cook pancetta in medium skillet over medium heat until brown, stirring often, about 8 minutes. Using slotted spoon, transfer pancetta to paper towels; drain. Pour off all but 2 tablespoons drippings from skillet. Add cream, garlic, and crushed pepper to drippings in skillet; bring to boil. Set cream mixture aside.

Heat oil in heavy large skillet over medium-high heat. Add zucchini; sauté until tender, stirring occasionally, about 10 minutes. Transfer to large plate. Season with salt and pepper. (*Pancetta, cream mixture, and zucchini can be made 2 hours ahead. Let stand at room temperature.*)

Cook pasta in large pot of boiling salted water until just tender but still firm to bite. Drain well. Return pasta to pot.

Meanwhile, place eggs in their shell in small bowl. Add enough hot water to cover. Let stand 5 minutes. Crack eggs into large bowl and whisk to blend. Bring cream mixture to boil in skillet. Gradually whisk hot cream mixture into eggs. Mix in ½ cup Parmesan cheese.

Add sauce to pasta and toss over medium heat until sauce coats pasta (do not boil). Add pancetta and zucchini; toss to heat through. Season with salt and pepper. Serve, passing remaining cheese.

6 SERVINGS

Casual Dinner for 6

Caesar Salad

Bucatini Carbonara with Zucchini
(*at left; pictured opposite*)

Montepulciano

Blood Orange Tart with Orange Caramel Sauce
(*page 168*)

Coffee

Farfalle and Tuna Casserole

2 6-ounce cans tuna, packed in oil
½ cup dry breadcrumbs
½ cup grated Parmesan cheese

1 pound farfalle (bow-tie pasta)
3 10-ounce containers purchased refrigerated Alfredo sauce
2 cups thinly sliced green onions
1 cup frozen peas, thawed
2 teaspoons dried oregano
2 teaspoons grated lemon peel
2 tablespoons fresh lemon juice

Preheat oven to 400°F. Drain tuna; reserve oil. Mix breadcrumbs and Parmesan in small bowl. Mix in 4 tablespoons reserved oil from tuna.

Cook pasta in pot of boiling salted water until just tender but still firm to bite, stirring occasionally. Drain well. Transfer pasta to large bowl. Mix in tuna and all remaining ingredients. Transfer pasta mixture to 3-quart oval baking dish. Sprinkle with crumb mixture. Bake until pasta is hot and topping is golden brown, about 25 minutes.

6 SERVINGS

Pasta with Sausage and Mushrooms

2½	pounds Italian sweet sausages, casings removed, crumbled
3	tablespoons olive oil
1½	pounds mushrooms, thickly sliced
3	cups chopped onions
1½	cups chopped fresh basil
¼	cup chopped fresh oregano
6	large garlic cloves, chopped
1	cup dry white wine
5	cups canned crushed tomatoes with added puree
2	cups diced tomatoes (about 4 medium-large tomatoes)
2	tablespoons (¼ stick) butter
1¼	pounds pappardelle or mafaldine pasta (or any wide, flat noodles)
1½	cups grated pecorino Romano cheese (about 4½ ounces)

Sauté sausage in heavy large pot over medium-high heat until brown, about 12 minutes. Using slotted spoon, transfer sausage to large bowl. Add oil to drippings in pot. Add mushrooms and onions; sauté until tender and brown, about 15 minutes. Stir in 1 cup chopped basil, oregano, and garlic; sauté 1 minute. Add wine; cook until almost absorbed, about 4 minutes. Add sausage and crushed tomatoes; cover and simmer over medium heat until thickened, about 25 minutes. Add diced tomatoes and butter; simmer until tomatoes are soft, stirring frequently, about 15 minutes. Season with salt and pepper. *(Can be made 1 day ahead. Cool slightly. Chill uncovered until cold, then cover and refrigerate. Bring to simmer before continuing.)*

Cook pasta in large pot of boiling salted water until tender but still firm to bite, stirring occasionally. Drain well; return to pot. Pour sauce over pasta; toss to coat. Add ½ cup cheese and ½ cup basil; toss to combine. Season with salt and pepper. Transfer pasta to serving dish. Serve, passing remaining cheese separately.

8 SERVINGS

Pappardelle Bolognese

¼ cup olive oil
2 slices thick-cut bacon, diced
1 cup chopped onion
½ cup chopped celery
½ cup chopped carrot
4 garlic cloves, minced
1 tablespoon chopped fresh thyme
1 pound ground veal
1 pound ground pork
1 cup dry red wine
2 bay leaves
2 14-ounce cans beef broth
1½ cups canned tomato puree

1 pound pappardelle or mafaldine pasta
Freshly grated Parmesan cheese

Heat oil in heavy large pot over medium-high heat. Add bacon; sauté until beginning to brown, about 6 minutes. Add onion, celery, carrot, garlic, and thyme; sauté 5 minutes. Add veal and pork; sauté until brown and cooked through, breaking up meat with back of fork, about 10 minutes. Add wine and bay leaves. Simmer until liquid is slightly reduced, about 10 minutes. Add broth and tomato puree. Reduce heat to medium-low; simmer until sauce thickens, stirring often, about 1 hour 15 minutes. Season with salt and pepper. (*Can be made 1 day ahead. Cool slightly. Refrigerate uncovered until cold, then cover and keep chilled. Bring to simmer before using.*)

Boil pasta in large pot of boiling salted water until just tender but still firm to bite, stirring often. Drain. Transfer to pot with sauce; toss. Serve with Parmesan.

4 TO 6 SERVINGS

Pizza Arizona

2 teaspoons yellow cornmeal
1 10-ounce tube refrigerated pizza dough
1½ cups purchased chipotle salsa
2 tablespoons olive oil
1½ teaspoons chili powder
1½ cups shredded Mexican-style four-cheese mix or pizza cheese
¼ cup chopped fresh cilantro

Position rack in bottom third of oven and preheat to 400°F. Sprinkle cornmeal on baking sheet. Unroll dough onto sheet, forming 10x15-inch rectangle.

Mix salsa, oil, and chili powder in small bowl. Toss cheese and cilantro in medium bowl. Spoon salsa mixture over dough, leaving ½-inch border. Sprinkle with cheese mixture. Bake pizza until crust is golden brown and cheese is melted and bubbling, about 15 minutes. Cut into squares and serve.

2 SERVINGS

Roasted Vegetable Pizza

1 10-ounce tube refrigerated pizza dough
4 tablespoons garlic-flavored olive oil or regular olive oil
8 cherry tomatoes, halved
1 red bell pepper, sliced
1 medium zucchini, quartered lengthwise, cut crosswise
    into ½-inch-thick pieces (about 1¾ cups)
1 small red onion, thinly sliced (about 2 cups)
1 8-ounce package shredded 3- or 4-cheese pizza blend
3 tablespoons chopped fresh basil

Position 1 rack in top third of oven and 1 rack in bottom third of oven; preheat to 425°F. Unroll pizza dough and place on heavy large baking sheet. Press or stretch to 13x9-inch rectangle. Brush with 1 tablespoon oil. Toss tomatoes, bell pepper, zucchini, and onion with remaining 3 tablespoons oil in large bowl. Arrange vegetables on large rimmed baking sheet. Place pizza crust on top rack in oven and vegetables on bottom rack. Bake until pizza crust is golden brown and vegetables are softened and brown in spots, about 13 minutes. Remove from oven. Sprinkle crust with cheese and top with vegetables. Top with basil and bake until cheese is melted and bubbly, about 3 minutes. Cut into squares and serve.

2 TO 4 SERVINGS

Mozzarella and Prosciutto Pizza with Balsamic Onions

DOUGH

- 1½ cups unbleached all purpose flour
- 1½ teaspoons coarse salt
- ½ cup warm water (105°F to 115°F)
- 1 teaspoon dry yeast
- 1½ tablespoons olive oil
- 1 tablespoon honey

TOPPINGS

- 2 tablespoons plus ½ cup olive oil
- 1 12-ounce red onion, thinly sliced
- 2 tablespoons balsamic vinegar
- 2 teaspoons Worcestershire sauce

- 4 large garlic cloves, chopped

- 1 large red bell pepper

  All purpose flour
- 1 cup (packed) coarsely grated whole-milk mozzarella cheese
- 3 tablespoons coarsely grated Parmesan cheese

- 4 thin slices prosciutto, sliced crosswise into thin strips
- 2 teaspoons chopped fresh thyme
  Balsamic vinegar

FOR DOUGH: Mix flour and salt in large bowl. Place ½ cup warm water in small bowl. Sprinkle yeast over water and stir to blend. Let stand until dissolved, about 10 minutes. Pour yeast mixture into bowl with flour. Add oil and honey. Using flexible spatula, stir until coarse dough forms. Knead dough in bowl with 1 hand until smooth and elastic, about 6 minutes. Cover bowl; let dough stand 30 minutes. Refrigerate dough in bowl, still covered, at least 2 hours (dough will rise very little). (*Can be made 2 days ahead; keep refrigerated.*)

FOR TOPPINGS: Heat 2 tablespoons oil in heavy medium skillet over medium-high heat. Add onion and sauté until golden, about 12 minutes. Add vinegar and Worcestershire sauce. Reduce heat to medium-low; simmer until liquid cooks away and onion is very tender, about 4 minutes; season onion with salt and pepper.

Heat remaining ½ cup oil in heavy small skillet over medium-low heat. Add garlic and sauté just until garlic begins to brown, about 4 minutes. Using slotted spoon, transfer garlic to custard cup. Pour oil into separate small bowl.

Char bell pepper over gas flame or in broiler until blackened on all sides. Enclose in paper bag; let stand 10 minutes. Peel, seed, and slice thinly. (*Onion, garlic, garlic oil, and pepper can be prepared 1 day ahead. Cover separately and refrigerate.*)

Place chilled dough ball on work surface. Cover with plastic wrap; let stand at room temperature until malleable, about 1 hour.

Position rack in bottom third of oven. Place heavy large baking sheet on rack (invert sheet if rimmed). Preheat oven to 500°F at least 30 minutes. Roll out dough on lightly floured surface to 12-inch round, allowing dough to rest a few minutes if it springs back. Sprinkle flour on pizza paddle or another rimless baking sheet. Slide under dough. Brush 1 tablespoon reserved garlic oil over dough, leaving ½-inch plain border. Sprinkle with mozzarella, then reserved garlic, and balsamic onion. Top with pepper strips in spoke pattern. Sprinkle with Parmesan. Slide knife under dough to loosen from paddle, if sticking.

Position paddle at far edge of hot baking sheet in oven. Tilt paddle and pull back slowly, allowing pizza to slide onto sheet. Bake 6 minutes. Rotate pizza half a turn. Bake until crust is deep brown, about 6 minutes longer. Arrange prosciutto atop pizza. Bake until prosciutto softens, about 30 seconds. Using paddle, transfer pizza to board. Sprinkle with thyme. Cut into 8 wedges. Serve, passing more vinegar and garlic oil separately.

4 SERVINGS

Grownups' Pizza
Party for 6

Assorted Brine-Cured Olives

**Arugula Salad with
Ricotta Salata and Lemon**
(page 148)

**Mozzarella and Prosciutto Pizza
with Balsamic Onions**
(at left; pictured opposite)

**Pizza Bianca with Goat Cheese
and Greens**
(page 132)

Chianti

Trio of Gelati
(page 216)

Purchased Biscotti

Espresso

Pizza Bianca with Goat Cheese and Greens

CRUST

¾ cup warm water (105°F to 115°F)

1½ teaspoons dry yeast (from 1 envelope)

1 tablespoon extra-virgin olive oil

1 teaspoon salt

1¾ cups (about) unbleached all purpose flour

SEASONED OIL

2 tablespoons extra-virgin olive oil

1 large garlic clove, minced

¼ teaspoon dried crushed red pepper

TOPPING

1 bunch Swiss chard (about 10 ounces), white ribs cut away

2 tablespoons extra-virgin olive oil

1 large garlic clove, minced

Yellow cornmeal

8 ounces whole-milk mozzarella cheese, coarsely grated

4 ounces soft fresh goat cheese, crumbled (about 1 cup)

FOR CRUST: Pour ¾ cup water into large bowl. Sprinkle yeast over; stir to blend. Let stand 10 minutes to dissolve yeast. Add oil and salt, then 1½ cups flour. Stir until well blended (dough will be sticky). Turn dough out onto floured surface and knead until smooth and elastic, adding just enough flour to prevent dough from sticking, about 5 minutes (dough will be soft). Shape dough into ball; place in large oiled bowl and turn to coat. Cover bowl with towel. Let rise at cool room temperature until almost doubled, about 2 hours. Punch dough down; form into ball. Return to bowl; cover with towel and let rise until doubled, about 3 hours.

MEANWHILE, PREPARE SEASONED OIL: Mix oil, garlic, and pepper in bowl. Let stand 1 hour.

FOR TOPPING: Cook chard in large pot of boiling salted water until just tender, about 2 minutes. Drain. Rinse under cold water; drain. Squeeze dry, then coarsely chop. Heat 2 tablespoons oil in small skillet over medium heat. Add garlic and stir 30 seconds. Add chard and stir 1 minute. Season to taste with salt.

Preheat oven to 500°F. Punch down dough. Form into ball; place on floured work surface. Cover with kitchen towel; let rest 30 minutes.

Sprinkle rimless baking sheet with cornmeal. Roll out dough on floured surface to 13-inch round. Transfer to baking sheet. Sprinkle mozzarella over dough, leaving 1-inch border. Scatter chard over mozzarella. Top with goat cheese. Brush crust edge with some of seasoned oil. Set aside 2 teaspoons seasoned oil; drizzle remaining oil over pizza.

Bake until crust is brown, about 15 minutes. Brush edge with seasoned oil and serve.

4 SERVINGS

State Fair Potato Salad
(page 159)

On the Side

Side Dishes

Salads

Breads

Roasted Asparagus with Fresh Favas and Morels

½ cup water
½ ounce dried morel mushrooms, rinsed
1 shallot, chopped
1 tablespoon Sherry vinegar

1 pound fresh fava beans, shelled (about 1 cup)

1½ pounds thick asparagus, trimmed
3 tablespoons olive oil

3 slices pancetta or bacon, chopped
2 teaspoons chopped fresh thyme

Bring ½ cup water to boil in small saucepan. Add mushrooms. Remove from heat. Place shallot in small bowl. Add vinegar. Let mixture stand 30 minutes.

Preheat oven to 450°F. Cook favas in large saucepan of boiling salted water until crisp-tender, about 2 minutes. Drain. Rinse under cold water. Drain. Remove and discard outer skin of each fava bean; transfer favas to medium bowl.

Place asparagus on large rimmed baking sheet. Drizzle with 1 tablespoon oil. Sprinkle asparagus with salt and pepper. Toss to coat. Roast asparagus until tender when pierced with skewer, about 20 minutes.

Meanwhile, drain mushrooms and slice thinly. Sauté pancetta in saucepan over medium heat until crisp, about 5 minutes. Add remaining 2 tablespoons oil and sliced mushrooms; sauté 2 minutes. Add shallot mixture; simmer 2 minutes. Add favas and toss to heat through. Stir in thyme. Season fava-mushroom mixture to taste with salt and pepper.

Place asparagus on platter. Top with fava-mushroom mixture and serve.

6 SERVINGS

SIDE DISHES

Jasmine Rice with Green Onions, Peas, and Lemon

1¾ cups water
1¼ cups jasmine rice, rinsed well, drained, or long-grain white rice
½ teaspoon salt

½ cup shelled fresh or frozen peas
2 tablespoons extra-virgin olive oil
6 green onions, thinly sliced
2 tablespoons fresh lemon juice
2 tablespoons chopped fresh parsley
1 tablespoon grated lemon peel

Combine 1¾ cups water, rice, and salt in large saucepan. Bring to boil over high heat. Reduce heat to low; cover and cook until rice is tender, about 15 minutes. Remove from heat. Let stand covered 15 minutes. Fluff with fork. Cool.

Cook peas in medium saucepan of boiling salted water 1 minute. Drain. Rinse under cold water. Drain.

Heat oil in large nonstick skillet over medium-high heat. Add all but 2 tablespoons green onions; sauté 30 seconds. Add rice and sauté until heated through, stirring to break pieces, about 4 minutes. Add peas, lemon juice, parsley, and lemon peel. Sauté 2 minutes to blend flavors. Transfer to serving bowl. Sprinkle with remaining green onions.

6 SERVINGS

Sautéed Baby Squash and Radishes with Marjoram

2 pounds assorted baby squash (such as baby zucchini, baby yellow crookneck, and baby pattypan), trimmed

2 tablespoons (¼ stick) butter
2 tablespoons olive oil
3 bunches radishes, trimmed, sliced
1 teaspoon chopped fresh marjoram

Cook all squash in large pot of boiling salted water 1 minute. Drain. Place squash in ice water to cool. Drain. (*Can be made 1 day ahead. Pat dry with paper towels; cover and chill.*)

Melt butter with oil in large skillet over medium-high heat. Add all squash; sauté until crisp-tender, 4 minutes. Add radishes and marjoram; stir 1 minute. Season with salt and pepper.

8 SERVINGS

Grilled Corn on the Cob with Maple-Chipotle Glaze

½ cup pure maple syrup

¼ cup (½ stick) butter

2 garlic cloves, minced

4 teaspoons minced canned chipotle chilies*

¼ teaspoon salt

6 ears fresh corn, husked

Bring first 5 ingredients to simmer in heavy small saucepan over medium heat. Reduce heat to low and simmer until glaze is reduced to ¾ cup, stirring occasionally, about 10 minutes. *(Glaze can be made 1 day ahead. Cover and refrigerate.)*

Prepare barbecue (medium heat). Brush corn with some of glaze. Grill until lightly charred in spots, turning frequently, about 8 minutes. Transfer corn to platter. Brush corn with remaining glaze. Sprinkle generously with salt and serve.

Chipotle chilies canned in a spicy tomato sauce, sometimes called adobo, *are available at Latin American markets and some supermarkets.*

6 SERVINGS

Broccoli with Sesame Seeds and Dried Red Pepper

3 tablespoons sesame seeds
¾ teaspoon kosher salt
¾ teaspoon dried crushed red pepper

1¼ pounds broccoli, cut into florets
1 tablespoon toasted sesame oil

Toast sesame seeds in heavy small skillet over medium heat until golden, about 5 minutes. Set aside 1 tablespoon toasted sesame seeds. Place remaining sesame seeds in spice grinder. Add salt and ½ teaspoon crushed red pepper; grind coarsely. Set sesame-red pepper mixture aside.

Steam broccoli until crisp-tender, about 7 minutes. Transfer to large bowl. Add oil, 1 tablespoon reserved sesame seeds, remaining ¼ teaspoon crushed red pepper, and 2 teaspoons sesame-red pepper mixture; toss to combine. Serve, passing remaining sesame-red pepper mixture separately.

4 SERVINGS

Grilled Eggplant with Yogurt-Mint Sauce

1 cup plain yogurt
3 tablespoons chopped fresh mint
2 tablespoons fresh lemon juice
1 teaspoon curry powder
1 teaspoon dried crushed red pepper

2 eggplants (each about 1 pound), cut crosswise into 1-inch-thick rounds
¼ cup oriental sesame oil
2 tablespoons coriander seeds, cracked

Mix first 5 ingredients in medium bowl; season with salt and pepper.

Prepare barbecue (medium-high heat). Rub eggplant rounds on both sides with sesame oil. Sprinkle with coriander, salt, and pepper. Grill until slightly charred, about 6 minutes per side.

Arrange eggplant rounds on platter. Serve with yogurt-mint sauce.

6 SERVINGS

Summer Succotash

3 tablespoons butter

3 tablespoons olive oil

1 large onion, chopped

1 red bell pepper, cut into ½-inch pieces

1 green bell pepper, cut into ½-inch pieces

1 garlic clove, minced

2 cups fresh corn kernels (from about 3 ears)

2 medium-size zucchini, trimmed, cut into ¾-inch pieces

2 medium-size yellow crookneck squash, trimmed, cut into ¾-inch pieces

1 10-ounce package frozen baby lima beans, thawed

4 tablespoons chopped fresh Italian parsley

1 tablespoon chopped fresh marjoram

Melt butter with oil in heavy large deep skillet over medium-high heat. Add onion, both bell peppers, and garlic; sauté until peppers are crisp-tender, about 5 minutes. Add corn, zucchini, yellow squash, and lima beans; sauté until vegetables are just tender, about 7 minutes longer. Stir in 3 tablespoons parsley and marjoram. Season to taste with salt and pepper. Transfer succotash to bowl. Sprinkle with remaining 1 tablespoon parsley and serve.

8 SERVINGS

Catch-of-the-Day Dinner for a Crowd

Parsley, Garlic, and Onion Spread
(page 18; double recipe)

Grilled Whole Fish with Olive Oil and Garlic
(page 92)

Summer Succotash
(at left; double recipe)

Tomato Gratin with White Cheddar Breadcrumbs
(page 144; triple recipe)

Baked Potatoes

Sauvignon Blanc

Strawberries

Chocolate Mint Cookies
(page 226)

Coffee

Tricolor Potatoes with Pesto and Parmesan

 8 tablespoons olive oil
 1 cup (packed) fresh basil leaves
 2 large shallots
 4 garlic cloves

 Nonstick vegetable oil spray
1½ pounds red-skinned new potatoes
1½ pounds Yukon Gold potatoes (each about 1½ inches in diameter)
 1 pound purple potatoes (each about 1½ inches in diameter)

 ¾ cup freshly grated Parmesan cheese

Puree 4 tablespoons olive oil, basil, shallots, and garlic in processor. Season sauce with salt and pepper. (*Can be made 8 hours ahead. Cover; chill.*)

Preheat oven to 400°F. Spray large baking sheet with nonstick spray. Toss all potatoes with 4 tablespoons olive oil, salt, and pepper in large bowl to coat. Transfer to prepared baking sheet. Roast potatoes until almost tender, about 35 minutes. Pour basil sauce over potatoes and toss to coat. Continue roasting potatoes until golden brown and tender when pierced with skewer, about 20 minutes longer.

Transfer potatoes to serving bowl. Add cheese and toss to coat.

10 SERVINGS

Green Beans with Citrus Butter Sauce

 1 pound green beans, trimmed
 1 tablespoon olive oil
 1 tablespoon grated orange peel
 2 teaspoons grated lemon peel
 2 garlic cloves, minced
 ¼ cup low-salt chicken broth
 2 tablespoons (¼ stick) butter

Cook beans in large pot of boiling salted water until crisp-tender, about 4 minutes. Drain well. Heat oil in heavy large skillet over medium-high heat. Add orange peel, lemon peel, and garlic; stir 1 minute. Add broth and simmer 1 minute. Add butter and beans. Toss until beans are heated through, about 2 minutes. Season with salt and pepper.

4 TO 6 SERVINGS

Tomato Gratin with White Cheddar Breadcrumbs

1 28-ounce can whole tomatoes, well drained
4 large garlic cloves, minced
3 tablespoons chopped fresh chives
2 tablespoons dry Marsala

1 cup fresh breadcrumbs made from French bread
1 cup grated white cheddar cheese
2 tablespoons extra-virgin olive oil

Preheat oven to 350°F. Mix tomatoes, garlic, 2½ tablespoons chives, and Marsala in bowl to blend; season to taste with salt and pepper. Transfer to 8-inch-diameter gratin dish with 1½-inch-high sides.

Mix breadcrumbs, cheese, and olive oil in large bowl to blend. Season topping to taste with salt and pepper. Sprinkle topping over tomatoes. Bake until juices bubble and topping is golden brown, about 40 minutes. Let stand 10 minutes. Sprinkle with remaining ½ tablespoon chives and serve.

4 TO 6 SERVINGS

Creamy Polenta with Gorgonzola and Spinach

4 cups low-salt chicken broth
2 garlic cloves, chopped
2 teaspoons chopped fresh rosemary
1½ cups polenta (coarse cornmeal)*
1 cup (packed) chopped fresh spinach
½ cup whipping cream
1 cup crumbled Gorgonzola cheese
3 tablespoons chopped fresh parsley

Bring first 3 ingredients to boil in large saucepan. Gradually whisk in polenta. Reduce heat and simmer until mixture thickens, stirring often, about 10 minutes. Add spinach and stir until wilted, about 2 minutes. Add cream and simmer until almost absorbed and polenta thickens, about 5 minutes. Add cheese and parsley; stir until cheese melts. Season to taste with salt and pepper. Transfer to bowl and serve.

Sold at Italian markets, natural foods stores, and some supermarkets.

4 TO 6 SERVINGS

Mashed Potatoes with Fontina and Italian Parsley

2	pounds medium-size russet potatoes
¾	cup half and half
2	tablespoons (¼ stick) butter
1¼	cups (packed) grated Fontina cheese (about 6 ounces)
3	tablespoons chopped fresh Italian parsley

Preheat oven to 375°F. Using small knife, pierce potatoes in several places. Place potatoes on baking sheet. Bake until tender when pierced with skewer, about 1 hour. Cool slightly.

Bring half and half to simmer in heavy small saucepan. Scrape potatoes from skin into large bowl. Using ricer, food mill, or potato masher, mash potatoes. Mix in half and half. Add butter; stir vigorously until butter melts and potatoes are smooth. Stir in ²/₃ of cheese and 3 tablespoons parsley. Season with salt and pepper. Transfer potatoes to 11x7x2-inch glass baking dish. Sprinkle with remaining cheese. *(Can be prepared 2 hours ahead. Cover and let stand at room temperature.)*

Preheat oven to 425°F. Bake potatoes until heated through and cheese melts, about 15 minutes.

6 SERVINGS

Romaine Salad with Chives and Blue Cheese

1 large head of romaine lettuce, torn into bite-size pieces
3 tablespoons olive oil
2½ tablespoons fresh lemon juice
1 shallot, minced
1 teaspoon Dijon mustard
1 bunch fresh chives, cut into 1½-inch-long pieces
1 cup crumbled blue cheese

Place lettuce in large bowl. Whisk oil, lemon juice, shallot, and mustard in small bowl to blend. Season dressing to taste with salt and pepper. Mix in chives. Drizzle dressing over lettuce and toss to coat. Sprinkle cheese over and serve.

6 SERVINGS

Spinach Salad with Oranges and Almonds

6 tablespoons vegetable oil
¼ cup fresh orange juice
3 green onions, minced
3 tablespoons unseasoned rice vinegar
1 tablespoon honey
1 tablespoon chopped fresh tarragon
1 teaspoon grated orange peel
4 oranges

1½ 6-ounce packages baby spinach
⅔ cup sliced almonds, toasted

Whisk first 7 ingredients in small bowl. Season with salt and pepper. Cut peel and white pith from oranges. Working over medium bowl, cut between membranes to release segments. *(Dressing and oranges can be prepared 1 day ahead. Cover separately and refrigerate. Rewhisk dressing before using.)*

Combine spinach, half of almonds, and all orange segments in large bowl with enough dressing to coat. Divide among 6 plates. Sprinkle with almonds.

6 SERVINGS

SALADS

Waldorf Salad with Cranberries and Pecans in Radicchio Cups

- 1 cup mayonnaise
- 1 teaspoon grated lemon peel
- 1 teaspoon fresh lemon juice

- 6 Granny Smith apples (about 2½ pounds), unpeeled, cored, cut into ½-inch pieces
- 1½ cups chopped celery
- 1½ cups chopped radishes
- ¾ cup dried cranberries
- ½ cup finely chopped red onion

- 2 cups watercress leaves
- 1½ cups pecans, toasted, chopped
- 2 heads of radicchio, leaves separated

Mix mayonnaise, lemon peel, and fresh lemon juice in medium bowl to blend. Season to taste with salt and pepper. Refrigerate 15 minutes.

Toss apples, celery, radishes, cranberries, and red onion in large bowl. Add lemon mayonnaise and toss to coat. *(Can be prepared up to 8 hours ahead. Cover and refrigerate.)*

Fold watercress and chopped pecans into salad. Arrange 2 radicchio leaves on each plate. Spoon salad into center of radicchio leaves and serve.

8 TO 10 SERVINGS

Arugula Salad with Ricotta Salata and Lemon

1   large shallot, minced (¼ cup)
2   tablespoons fresh lemon juice
3   tablespoons extra-virgin olive oil

10 cups loosely packed arugula
1   medium fennel bulb, trimmed, halved lengthwise, cored, very thinly sliced
3   ounces ricotta salata or pecorino Romano, shaved into long strips with vegetable peeler

Whisk shallot and lemon juice in small bowl to blend. Gradually whisk in oil. Season to taste with salt and pepper. Let stand 15 minutes to blend flavors.

Combine arugula and sliced fennel in large bowl. Toss with enough dressing to coat salad. Add shaved cheese; toss gently and serve.

6 SERVINGS

Chopped Salad with Feta, Green Onions, and Pine Nuts

¼ cup red wine vinegar
2 tablespoons balsamic vinegar
1 tablespoon Dijon mustard
1 teaspoon dried Italian seasoning
½ cup olive oil

1 large head of romaine lettuce, chopped
6 large green onions, chopped
1 large red bell pepper, chopped
1 large yellow bell pepper, chopped
1½ cups crumbled feta cheese
1⅓ cups pine nuts, toasted
½ cup chopped fresh dill

Whisk first 4 ingredients in small bowl to blend. Gradually whisk in oil. Season dressing to taste with salt and pepper.

Combine lettuce, green onions, bell peppers, feta cheese, pine nuts, and dill in large bowl. Add dressing; toss to coat.

8 SERVINGS

Apricot, Berry, and Jicama Salad with Honey-Lime Dressing

8 ounces apricots or nectarines, halved, pitted, cut into ½-inch pieces
1 1-pint basket strawberries, hulled, cut into ½-inch pieces
1 ½-pint basket fresh blueberries
1 ½-pint basket fresh raspberries
1½ cups ½-inch pieces peeled jicama
2 teaspoons minced seeded jalapeño chili
3 tablespoons fresh lime juice
3 tablespoons honey
1 tablespoon vegetable oil
2 tablespoons roasted salted sunflower seeds

Combine first 6 ingredients in large bowl. Whisk lime juice, honey, and oil in small bowl to blend. Season to taste with salt and pepper. Pour dressing over fruit mixture; toss gently to coat. Divide salad among 6 plates. Sprinkle with sunflower seeds and serve.

6 SERVINGS

Roasted Green Bean, Red Onion, and Beet Salad

        10   large beets, trimmed
         6   tablespoons extra-virgin olive oil
         8   teaspoons chopped fresh thyme

             Nonstick vegetable oil spray
         4   red onions, each cut into 6 wedges

        2½   pounds slender green beans, trimmed, cut into 3-inch lengths
        ¼   cup water

         3   tablespoons balsamic vinegar

Preheat oven to 400°F. Wrap beets tightly in foil. Place directly on oven rack. Roast until tender when pierced with knife, about 1 hour. Cool beets. Peel and quarter beets. Transfer to large bowl. Add 2 tablespoons olive oil, 2 teaspoons thyme, salt, and pepper; toss to coat.

Spray 2 large rimmed baking sheets with nonstick spray. Divide onion wedges between prepared baking sheets. Brush onions on both sides with 2 tablespoons oil; sprinkle with 4 teaspoons thyme. Sprinkle with salt and pepper. Arrange onions cut side down and roast until golden brown on bottom, about 10 minutes. Turn onions over. Roast until golden brown and tender, about 10 minutes longer. Transfer to another large bowl.

Divide green beans between same baking sheets. Drizzle beans with remaining 2 tablespoons olive oil, ¼ cup water, and 2 teaspoons thyme. Sprinkle with salt and pepper. Cover tightly with foil and roast until almost crisp-tender, about 14 minutes. Uncover and continue to roast until water evaporates and beans are crisp-tender, about 5 minutes. Transfer to bowl with onions. *(Beets, onions, and green beans can be prepared 2 hours ahead. Let stand at room temperature.)*

Drizzle onions and green beans with balsamic vinegar; toss to coat. Season to taste with salt and pepper. Top with beets and serve warm or at room temperature.

10 SERVINGS

Buffet Dinner for 10

Orange Blossom Cocktail
(page 41)

Brie and Chive Toasts with Arugula
(page 13)

Roasted Salmon with Corn Relish
(page 88)

Tricolor Potatoes with Pesto and Parmesan
(page 143)

Roasted Green Bean, Red Onion, and Beet Salad
(at left; pictured opposite)

Rioja or Sangiovese

Raspberry Cake with Marsala, Crème Fraîche, and Raspberries
(page 196)

Warm Goat Cheese Salad with Grilled Olive Bread

VINAIGRETTE

2 garlic cloves, peeled, halved

¼ cup extra-virgin olive oil

1 tablespoon chopped fresh basil

2 tablespoons red wine vinegar

2 tablespoons Dijon mustard

SALAD

1 cup panko (Japanese breadcrumbs)*

1 tablespoon chopped fresh thyme

1 tablespoon chopped fresh parsley

1 tablespoon chopped fresh basil

½ teaspoon ground black pepper

¼ teaspoon salt

3 4-ounce logs soft fresh goat cheese, each halved crosswise, halves pressed
 to ½-inch thickness

2 large egg whites, lightly beaten until foamy

1 tablespoon olive oil

6 ¾-inch-thick slices olive bread
 Additional olive oil

2 5-ounce packages mixed baby greens

FOR VINAIGRETTE: Place garlic and oil in small glass measuring cup or ramekin. Cover tightly with plastic wrap and microwave 30 seconds. Transfer garlic to small bowl. Reserve oil. Using fork, coarsely mash garlic. Add basil, vinegar, and mustard to mashed garlic. Whisk until smooth. Gradually whisk in reserved garlic oil. Season to taste with salt and pepper. (*Can be made 1 day ahead. Cover and refrigerate. Let stand 1 hour at room temperature and rewhisk before using.*)

FOR SALAD: Mix first 6 ingredients in medium bowl to blend. Dip each cheese round into egg whites, turning to coat. Coat each with breadcrumb mixture. Transfer coated cheese rounds to plate. Cover with plastic and chill at least 1 hour and up to 8 hours.

 Prepare barbecue (medium-high heat). Heat 1 tablespoon olive oil in heavy large non-stick skillet over medium-high heat. Add cheese rounds and cook until golden and crisp, about 3 minutes per side. Transfer to plate. Brush bread slices on both sides with olive oil. Grill until beginning to toast, about 3 minutes per side. Transfer to plate. Place greens in large bowl and toss with all but 2 tablespoons vinaigrette; season to taste with salt and pepper. Divide salad among 6 plates. Top each with 1 cheese round and 1 slice grilled bread. Drizzle cheese rounds with 2 tablespoons vinaigrette and serve.

Available at Asian markets and in the Asian foods section of some supermarkets.

6 SERVINGS

Asian Noodle, Mushroom, and Cabbage Salad

12 large dried shiitake mushrooms

1 tablespoon peanut oil
3 cups thinly sliced Napa cabbage
1 tablespoon minced peeled fresh ginger
1 tablespoon minced garlic
14 green onions; 12 halved lengthwise and cut on diagonal into 2-inch lengths, 2 chopped
3 tablespoons soy sauce

1 1-pound package fresh thin Chinese egg noodles or one 12-ounce package dried Chinese egg noodles
⅓ cup oriental sesame oil
2 tablespoons fresh lemon juice
1 tablespoon unseasoned rice vinegar
2 teaspoons sugar
3 hard-boiled eggs; 2 thinly sliced, 1 chopped for garnish
1 cup chopped fresh cilantro

Place mushrooms in medium bowl; add enough boiling water to cover. Let stand until softened, about 45 minutes. Drain mushrooms. Cut off stems and discard; thinly slice caps.

Heat peanut oil in heavy large wok or nonstick skillet over medium-high heat. Add cabbage, ginger, garlic, and mushrooms. Stir-fry until cabbage wilts, about 2 minutes. Add 2-inch green onion pieces; toss until green tops begin to wilt, about 30 seconds. Remove from heat. Mix in 1 tablespoon soy sauce.

Cook noodles in large pot of boiling salted water until just tender but still firm to bite. Drain well; place in large bowl. Whisk sesame oil, next 3 ingredients, and 2 tablespoons soy sauce in small bowl. Add to noodles. Add sliced eggs, ¾ cup cilantro, and cabbage mixture; toss to blend well. Season with salt and pepper. (*Can be made 1 day ahead. Cover and chill, tossing occasionally.*)

Sprinkle salad with 2 chopped green onions, chopped egg, and remaining ¼ cup cilantro.

8 SERVINGS

Watermelon and Watercress Salad with Ginger

2	tablespoons rice vinegar
1½	tablespoons vegetable oil
2	teaspoons minced peeled fresh ginger
1½	teaspoons grated lime peel
1	garlic clove, minced
2	cups ½-inch pieces peeled seedless watermelon
1	large bunch watercress, thick stems trimmed (about 2 cups packed)
1	cup ½-inch pieces peeled seeded cucumber (about ½ large)
4	green onions, thinly sliced diagonally
¼	cup chopped fresh cilantro

Whisk vinegar, oil, ginger, lime peel, and garlic in large bowl to blend. Season to taste with salt and pepper. Add watermelon and all remaining ingredients to bowl with dressing and toss to coat. Divide salad among 4 plates and serve.

4 SERVINGS

South-of-the-Border Coleslaw with Cilantro and Jalapeño

     4 cups thinly sliced green cabbage (from about ½ large head)
     1 red bell pepper, thinly sliced
     ½ cup chopped fresh cilantro
     1 small jalapeño chili, seeded, minced
     3 tablespoons olive oil
     2 tablespoons fresh lime juice
     1½ teaspoons ground cumin

Combine cabbage, bell pepper, cilantro, and jalapeño in large bowl; toss to blend. Whisk oil, lime juice, and cumin in small bowl to blend. Pour dressing over cabbage mixture. Season to taste with salt and pepper. (*Can be prepared 2 hours ahead. Cover and refrigerate. Toss before serving.*)

4 SERVINGS

Fresh Fennel Salad with Lemon and Parmesan

    3 large fresh fennel bulbs, trimmed, quartered, cored, very thinly sliced (about 9 cups)
  4½ tablespoons extra-virgin olive oil
  4½ tablespoons fresh lemon juice
   ¾ cup coarsely grated Parmesan cheese (about 2½ ounces)

       Fresh fennel fronds

Place fennel slices in large bowl. Drizzle with olive oil and lemon juice; toss to coat. Season generously with salt and pepper. Mix in grated cheese. Let stand at room temperature up to 1 hour or refrigerate up to 3 hours, tossing occasionally.

Transfer salad to serving bowl. Garnish with fennel fronds and serve.

8 SERVINGS

State Fair Potato Salad

3½ pounds red-skinned potatoes, peeled, cut into ¾-inch pieces
¼ cup juices from jar of sweet pickles

¾ cup mayonnaise
⅓ cup buttermilk
4 teaspoons Dijon mustard
1 teaspoon sugar
½ teaspoon ground black pepper
3 hard-boiled eggs, peeled, chopped
½ cup chopped red onion
½ cup chopped celery
½ cup chopped sweet pickles

Cook potatoes in large pot of boiling salted water until just tender, about 10 minutes. Drain; transfer to large bowl. Drizzle pickle juices over potatoes and toss gently. Cool to room temperature.

Whisk mayonnaise and next 4 ingredients in medium bowl. Pour over potatoes. Add eggs, onion, celery, and pickles; toss gently. Season with salt. *(Can be made 8 hours ahead. Chill. Serve at room temperature.)*

6 TO 8 SERVINGS

Chickpea Salad with Parsley, Lemon, and Sun-Dried Tomatoes

¼ cup olive oil
1 tablespoon cumin seeds

2 15½-ounce cans garbanzo beans (chickpeas), rinsed, drained
1 cucumber, peeled, seeded, chopped (about 1⅓ cups)
½ cup chopped fresh parsley
⅓ cup thinly sliced drained oil-packed sun-dried tomatoes
¼ cup fresh lemon juice
1 garlic clove, minced
¼ teaspoon dried crushed red pepper

Combine oil and cumin seeds in heavy small saucepan. Cook over medium heat 5 minutes to blend flavors, stirring occasionally. Cool.

Combine remaining ingredients in large bowl. Add cumin oil and toss to blend. Season salad to taste with salt and pepper. *(Can be made 1 day ahead. Cover and chill. Bring to room temperature before serving.)*

6 SERVINGS

Indian Dinner for 6

Tandoori-Spiced Chicken with Tomato-Ginger Chutney
(page 79)

Grilled Eggplant with Yogurt-Mint Sauce
(page 140)

Chickpea Salad with Parsley, Lemon, and Sun-Dried Tomatoes
(at left)

Indian Beer or Pale Ale

Chai Pots de Crème
(page 215)

Lemon-Poppy Seed Scones

        3 cups all purpose flour
        1 cup plus 1 tablespoon sugar
        3 tablespoons poppy seeds
        1 tablespoon baking powder
        2 teaspoons grated lemon peel
        1 teaspoon salt
       10 tablespoons (1¼ sticks) chilled unsalted butter, cut into small pieces
        1 large egg
        2 tablespoons fresh lemon juice
       ⅓ cup (or more) whole milk

Preheat oven to 375°F. Position rack in top third of oven. Mix flour, 1 cup sugar, poppy seeds, baking powder, lemon peel, and salt in processor. Add butter and cut in, using on/off turns, until mixture resembles coarse meal. Whisk egg and lemon juice in medium bowl to blend. Add to flour mixture. Using on/off turns, process until moist clumps form. Add ⅓ cup milk. Using on/off turns, process just until dough comes together, adding more milk if dough seems dry. Using floured hands, gather dough into ball. Flatten into 8-inch round. Cut round into 8 wedges. Transfer scones to large baking sheet; brush with milk. Sprinkle with remaining 1 tablespoon sugar. Bake until scones are golden brown and tester inserted into center comes out clean, about 25 minutes. Transfer to rack and cool. (*Can be made 1 day ahead. Store airtight at room temperature.*)

MAKES 8

Country-Style Bread

        2 cups warm water (110°F to 115°F)
        2 envelopes dry yeast
        1 tablespoon salt
        5 cups (about) bread flour

Pour 2 cups warm water into large bowl. Sprinkle yeast over; stir to blend. Let stand until yeast dissolves, about 7 minutes. Mix in salt, then 4½ cups flour, ½ cup at a time. Using flexible rubber spatula, knead dough in bowl by lifting dough edges and pressing into center, turning all of dough over occasionally and slowly rotating bowl, until sticky dough forms, about 8 minutes. Scrape down sides of bowl; cover with plastic wrap and let dough rise in warm draft-free area until doubled in volume, about 45 minutes. Using spatula, stir dough down. Cover; let rise again until doubled in volume, about 1 hour.

Sprinkle work surface with flour. Scrape dough out onto flour. Turning dough over and over in flour and sprinkling with more flour by tablespoonfuls if too sticky, shape into

14x3½-inch loaf. Sprinkle 18x12x1-inch baking sheet with flour. Transfer dough to prepared sheet. Cover loosely with plastic; let rise until doubled in volume, about 40 minutes.

Preheat oven to 375°F. Fill clean spray bottle with water. Gently pull plastic wrap off dough. Place bread in oven; immediately spray oven floor and walls generously with water. Bake bread 5 minutes. Spray oven generously with water again. Bake bread until golden and crusty all over, spraying oven with water 1 more time, about 35 minutes longer. Transfer bread to rack. Cool at least 30 minutes.

MAKES 1 LOAF

Dill Bread

- ¼ cup warm water (105°F to 115°F)
- 1 envelope dry yeast
- 1 cup whole-milk cottage cheese, room temperature
- ¼ cup chopped fresh dill
- 1 large egg
- 1 tablespoon unsalted butter, melted
- 1½ teaspoons salt
- 1 teaspoon sugar
- 1 teaspoon dill seeds
- 2¼ cups unbleached all purpose flour

Pour ¼ cup warm water into large bowl; sprinkle yeast over. Stir to blend. Let stand until yeast dissolves, about 10 minutes. Whisk in cottage cheese, chopped dill, egg, butter, salt, sugar, and dill seeds. Add 2¼ cups flour, ½ cup at a time, stirring until semi-stiff dough forms (do not knead). Cover bowl with plastic. Let dough rise in warm area until doubled, about 1 hour.

Butter 8-inch-diameter cake pan with 1½-inch-high sides. Punch down bread dough. Form into 6-inch round. Transfer dough round to prepared cake pan. Let dough rise uncovered in warm draft-free area until almost doubled in volume, about 45 minutes.

Position rack in center of oven and preheat to 350°F. Bake until bread is golden and sounds hollow when tapped, about 40 minutes. Turn bread out of pan; transfer to rack and cool completely. *(Can be made ahead. Wrap in foil, then resealable plastic bag, and let stand at room temperature 1 day or freeze up to 2 weeks. Thaw at room temperature.)*

MAKES 1 LOAF

Sharp Cheddar Cheese Biscuits

    4   cups unbleached all purpose flour
    8   teaspoons baking powder
    2   teaspoons sugar
    1   teaspoon salt
    1   cup (2 sticks) chilled unsalted butter, cut into ½-inch cubes
 1¾   cups (about) chilled whipping cream
    2   cups (packed) grated sharp cheddar cheese (about 8 ounces)

Preheat oven to 425°F. Blend flour, baking powder, sugar, and 1 teaspoon salt in processor. Add butter and cut in, using on/off turns, until mixture resembles coarse meal. Add 1½ cups cream. Blend until dough comes together in moist clumps, adding more cream by tablespoonfuls if dough is dry. Transfer to large bowl; gently mix in cheese.

Turn dough out onto lightly floured surface. Knead dough 30 seconds to bring together. Pat out to 1-inch thickness. Using 2-inch round cookie cutter, cut out biscuits. Gather scraps, pat dough out, and cut out more biscuits until all of dough is used.

Transfer biscuits to 2 large ungreased baking sheets, spacing apart. Bake until puffed and golden, about 15 minutes. Transfer to rack and cool. (*Can be made 6 hours ahead. Cool completely, cover, and let stand at room temperature.*)

MAKES ABOUT 24

Skillet Corn Bread with Red Bell Pepper

  1 medium-size red bell pepper

      Solid vegetable shortening

  1 cup unbleached all purpose flour

  1 cup yellow cornmeal

  2 tablespoons sugar

  2 teaspoons baking powder

 ¾ teaspoon salt

 ½ cup buttermilk

 ½ cup canned creamed corn

 ¼ cup (½ stick) unsalted butter, melted, cooled slightly

  1 large egg

 ½ teaspoon hot pepper sauce

  2 green onions, trimmed, sliced

Char bell pepper over gas flame or in broiler until blackened on all sides. Enclose in paper bag 10 minutes. Peel and seed pepper; cut into ⅓-inch-wide strips. Set aside.

Position rack in center of oven; preheat to 400°F. Generously coat 10-inch-diameter ovenproof skillet with vegetable shortening. Whisk flour, cornmeal, sugar, baking powder, and salt in large bowl to blend. Whisk buttermilk, creamed corn, melted butter, egg, and hot pepper sauce in medium bowl to blend. Add buttermilk mixture to dry ingredients and stir just until moistened. Transfer batter to prepared skillet. Arrange bell pepper strips in spoke pattern atop batter. Sprinkle with sliced green onions.

Bake corn bread until tester inserted into center comes out clean, about 20 minutes. Cool 15 minutes. Serve bread warm from skillet.

6 SERVINGS

Ultimate Sticky Buns

DOUGH

   1   cup warm water (105°F to 115°F)

   4   teaspoons dry yeast

 ²⁄₃   cup sugar

 ½   cup (1 stick) unsalted butter, room temperature

 ½   cup dry nonfat milk powder

1¼   teaspoons salt

   2   large eggs

4¼   cups (or more) all purpose flour

GLAZE

1¼   cups (packed) golden brown sugar

 ¾   cup (1½ sticks) unsalted butter, room temperature

 ¼   cup honey

 ¼   cup dark corn syrup

 ¼   cup water

   2   cups pecan halves

   4   teaspoons sugar

   4   teaspoons ground cinnamon

FOR DOUGH: Mix ¼ cup warm water, yeast, and pinch of sugar in small bowl. Let stand until foamy, about 8 minutes. Using electric mixer, beat remaining sugar, butter, milk powder, and salt in large bowl until well blended. Beat in eggs 1 at a time. Mix in remaining ¾ cup warm water and yeast mixture, then 3 cups flour, 1 cup at a time. Using rubber spatula, mix in 1 cup flour, scraping down sides of bowl frequently (dough will be soft and sticky). Sprinkle ¼ cup flour onto work surface. Turn dough out onto work surface and knead until smooth and elastic, adding more flour if sticky, about 8 minutes.

Butter another large bowl. Add dough; turn to coat. Cover bowl with plastic wrap and let dough rise in warm area until doubled, about 2½ hours.

FOR GLAZE: Butter two 10-inch round cake pans with 2-inch-high sides. Beat brown sugar, ½ cup butter, honey, corn syrup, and ¼ cup water in medium bowl to blend. Spread half of glaze in bottom of each prepared pan. Sprinkle 1 cup pecans over each.

Punch down dough. Divide dough in half. Roll each dough piece out on floured work surface to 12x9-inch rectangle. Brush any excess flour off dough. Spread remaining butter over dough rectangles, dividing equally. Mix 4 teaspoons sugar and cinnamon in small bowl. Sprinkle cinnamon sugar over rectangles. Starting at 1 long side, tightly roll up each rectangle into log. Cut each log into 12 rounds. Place 12 rounds, cut side down, in each prepared pan, spacing evenly. Cover tightly with plastic wrap. (*Can be prepared 1 day ahead; refrigerate.*) Let buns rise in warm area until almost doubled, about 1 hour (or 1 hour 25 minutes if refrigerated).

Preheat oven to 375°F. Bake buns until deep golden brown, about 30 minutes. Run small knife around pan sides to loosen sticky buns. Turn hot buns out onto platter. Cool about 30 minutes and serve.

MAKES 24

Irish Soda Bread with Raisins and Caraway

   5 cups all purpose flour
   1 cup sugar
   1 tablespoon baking powder
1½ teaspoons salt
   1 teaspoon baking soda
   ½ cup (1 stick) unsalted butter, cut into cubes, room temperature
2½ cups raisins
   3 tablespoons caraway seeds
2½ cups buttermilk
   1 large egg

Preheat oven to 350°F. Generously butter heavy ovenproof 10- to 12-inch-diameter skillet with 2- to 2¹/₂-inch-high sides. Whisk first 5 ingredients in large bowl to blend. Add butter; using fingertips, rub in until coarse crumbs form. Stir in raisins and caraway seeds. Whisk buttermilk and egg in medium bowl to blend. Add buttermilk mixture to dough; using wooden spoon, stir just until well incorporated (dough will be very sticky).

Transfer dough to prepared skillet; smooth top, mounding slightly in center. Using small sharp knife dipped into flour, cut 1-inch-deep X in top center of dough. Bake until bread is cooked through and tester inserted into center comes out clean, about 1 hour 15 minutes. Cool bread in skillet 10 minutes. Turn out onto rack and cool completely. (*Can be made 1 day ahead. Wrap tightly in aluminum foil; store at room temperature.*)

8 TO 10 SERVINGS

Blueberry Tartlets with Lime Curd
(page 174)

Desserts

Pies & Tarts

Fruit Desserts

Cakes

Mousses & Puddings

Frozen Desserts

Cookies

Blood Orange Tart with Orange Caramel Sauce

ORANGE CURD

1½ cups sugar

⅓ cup fresh blood orange juice

⅓ cup fresh lemon juice

6 large eggs

2 large egg yolks

1 tablespoon grated blood orange peel

½ cup (1 stick) unsalted butter, cut into 8 pieces, room temperature

CRUST

1½ cups all purpose flour

2 tablespoons sugar

¼ teaspoon salt

½ cup (1 stick) chilled unsalted butter, cut into 8 pieces

2 tablespoons whipping cream

1 large egg yolk

8 blood oranges

Orange Caramel Sauce (see recipe on next page)

FOR ORANGE CURD: Whisk sugar, orange juice, lemon juice, eggs, egg yolks, and orange peel in medium metal bowl to blend. Add butter; set bowl over saucepan of simmering water and whisk constantly until curd thickens and instant-read thermometer inserted into curd registers 175°F, about 12 minutes (do not boil). Remove bowl from over water. Press plastic wrap directly onto surface of curd; chill at least 1 day and up to 3 days.

FOR CRUST: Blend flour, sugar, and salt in processor. Add butter and cut in, using on/off turns, until mixture resembles coarse meal. Add cream and egg yolk and process until dough clumps together. Gather dough into ball; flatten into disk. Roll out dough on floured surface to 13-inch round. Transfer to 10-inch-diameter tart pan with removable bottom. Fold dough overhang in and press onto pan sides, forming double-thick sides. Pierce crust all over with fork; freeze 30 minutes.

Preheat oven to 375°F. Bake crust until cooked through, about 30 minutes. Cool crust completely in pan on rack. Spread curd evenly in cooled crust. *(Can be made 1 day ahead. Cover; chill.)*

Cut peel and white pith from oranges. Using small sharp knife, cut between membranes to release orange segments. Transfer segments to paper towels and pat dry. Arrange orange segments in concentric circles atop orange curd. Chill tart up to 1 hour.

Remove pan sides. Cut tart into wedges. Drizzle lightly with Orange Caramel Sauce and serve.

10 TO 12 SERVINGS

Orange Caramel Sauce

- ²⁄₃ cup sugar
- ¼ cup water
- ½ cup fresh blood orange juice
- ½ teaspoon grated blood orange peel

Combine sugar and ¼ cup water in heavy small saucepan. Stir over medium-low heat until sugar dissolves. Increase heat and boil without stirring until deep amber color, occasionally brushing down pan sides with wet pastry brush and swirling pan, about 8 minutes. Carefully add orange juice and orange peel (mixture will bubble vigorously). Stir over low heat until smooth and any caramel bits dissolve. Cool completely. *(Sauce can be prepared 1 day ahead. Cover and let sauce stand at room temperature.)*

MAKES ABOUT ²⁄₃ CUP

Berry Streusel Pie

CRUST

2¼ cups all purpose flour

1 tablespoon sugar

½ teaspoon salt

7 tablespoons chilled unsalted butter, cut into ½-inch cubes

⅓ cup chilled solid vegetable shortening, cut into ½-inch cubes

6 tablespoons (about) ice water

TOPPING

6 tablespoons (packed) golden brown sugar

6 tablespoons whole almonds

6 tablespoons (¾ stick) chilled unsalted butter, cut into ½-inch cubes

4½ tablespoons old-fashioned oats

4½ tablespoons all purpose flour

FILLING

1 cup sugar

¼ cup quick-cooking tapioca

2 tablespoons fresh lemon juice

5 cups assorted fresh berries (such as raspberries, blackberries, and blueberries; about 8 ounces of each)

FOR CRUST: Blend flour, sugar, and salt in processor. Add butter and shortening; using on/off turns, cut in until mixture resembles coarse meal. Add 5 tablespoons ice water and process until moist clumps form, adding more water by teaspoonfuls if mixture is dry. Gather dough into ball; flatten into disk. Wrap in plastic and chill at least 1 hour.

FOR TOPPING: Combine all ingredients in processor. Process until moist clumps form. *(Dough and topping can be made 1 day ahead. Cover topping and chill; keep dough chilled. Soften dough slightly at room temperature before rolling out.)*

FOR FILLING: Mix sugar, tapioca, and lemon juice in large bowl. Add berries and toss gently to combine. Let stand until tapioca softens slightly, stirring occasionally, about 45 minutes.

Preheat oven to 400°F. Roll out dough on lightly floured surface to 15-inch round. Transfer to 9-inch-diameter glass pie dish. Trim dough overhang to 1 inch. Fold overhang under and crimp decoratively, forming high-standing rim. Freeze crust 20 minutes.

Spoon filling into crust. Crumble topping evenly over filling. Bake pie until crust and topping are golden brown and filling is bubbling, covering loosely with sheet of foil if topping browns too quickly, about 55 minutes. Transfer pie to rack and cool at least 3 hours. *(Can be made 8 hours ahead. Let stand at room temperature.)* Cut pie into wedges and serve.

8 SERVINGS

Lemon and Toasted-Coconut Meringue Pie

CRUST

1½ cups all purpose flour

½ cup sweetened flaked coconut

¼ teaspoon salt

¾ cup (1½ sticks) chilled unsalted butter, cut into ½-inch pieces

1 large egg yolk

3 tablespoons (about) ice water

FILLING

1 cup sugar

2 tablespoons cornstarch

6 large egg yolks

4 large eggs

¾ cup fresh lemon juice

Pinch of salt

¾ cup (1½ sticks) unsalted butter, cut into ½-inch pieces

MERINGUE

6 large egg whites

¼ teaspoon cream of tartar

1⅓ cups powdered sugar

1 cup sweetened flaked coconut, lightly toasted

FOR CRUST: Blend flour, coconut, and salt in processor. Add butter and cut in, using on/off turns, until mixture resembles coarse meal. Whisk egg yolk and 2 tablespoons ice water in small bowl to blend. Add to processor and blend until mixture begins to clump together, adding more ice water by teaspoonfuls if dough is dry. Gather dough into ball; flatten into disk. Wrap in plastic; refrigerate 2 hours. *(Can be prepared 2 days ahead. Keep refrigerated. Soften slightly at room temperature before rolling.)*

Roll out dough on floured surface to 13-inch round. Transfer to 10-inch-diameter glass pie dish. Fold overhang under; crimp decoratively. Pierce crust all over with fork; freeze 30 minutes.

Preheat oven to 375°F. Line crust with foil; fill with dried beans or pie weights. Bake until crust is set, about 20 minutes. Remove foil and beans. Bake until crust is pale golden, about 15 minutes longer. Cool completely on rack.

FOR FILLING: Preheat oven to 300°F. Whisk sugar and cornstarch in heavy medium saucepan to blend. Whisk in yolks, whole eggs, lemon juice, and salt. Whisk over medium heat until mixture thickens and just begins to boil around edges, about 6 minutes. Add butter; whisk until smooth. Cool 10 minutes. Pour warm filling into crust.

FOR MERINGUE: Using electric mixer, beat egg whites in large bowl until foamy. Add cream of tartar and 1 tablespoon powdered sugar and beat until soft peaks form. Beat in remaining sugar, 1 tablespoon at a time, then beat until stiff glossy peaks form, about 7 minutes. Gently fold ¾ cup toasted coconut into meringue. Spread coconut meringue over warm filling, covering completely, sealing meringue to crust edges and mounding in center.

Bake pie 30 minutes. Reduce oven temperature to 275°F; bake 30 minutes longer. Sprinkle remaining ¼ cup toasted coconut over pie; continue to bake until meringue is light golden brown and set when pie is shaken slightly, about 15 minutes longer. Transfer pie to rack and cool completely, about 4 hours. *(Can be made 1 day ahead. Refrigerate uncovered.)*

10 SERVINGS

Blueberry Tartlets with Lime Curd

CURD

½ cup sugar

⅓ cup fresh lime juice

4 large egg yolks

5 tablespoons unsalted butter, cut into ½-inch cubes

1½ teaspoons grated lime peel

CRUST

1½ cups all purpose flour

3 tablespoons sugar

¼ teaspoon salt

½ cup (1 stick) chilled unsalted butter, cut into ½-inch cubes

3 tablespoons (about) chilled whipping cream

1 large egg yolk

TOPPING

3 ½-pint baskets blueberries

1 tablespoon sugar

FOR CURD: Whisk sugar and lime juice in heavy medium saucepan to blend. Whisk in yolks, then butter. Cook over medium-low heat until thick, smooth, and just beginning to bubble, stirring constantly, about 8 minutes. Remove from heat. Mix in lime peel. Transfer to small bowl. Press plastic wrap onto surface of curd. Refrigerate until cold, at least 4 hours. (*Can be made 4 days ahead. Keep refrigerated.*)

FOR CRUST: Blend flour, sugar, and salt in processor 5 seconds. Add butter and cut in, using on/off turns, until mixture resembles coarse meal. Add 2 tablespoons cream and egg yolk. Using on/off turns, blend until moist clumps form, adding more cream by teaspoonfuls if dough is dry. Shape dough into log. Cut crosswise into 8 equal rounds. Press each round over bottom and up sides of 3¾x¾-inch tartlet pan with removable bottom. Pierce crusts with fork. Chill at least 1 hour and up to 1 day.

FOR TOPPING: Place ½ cup berries and sugar in heavy small saucepan. Using fork, mash berries coarsely. Cook mixture over medium heat until beginning to simmer, stirring often, about 5 minutes. Using rubber spatula, push as much of mixture as possible through strainer set over medium bowl. Mix remaining berries into strained berries. Set aside.

Preheat oven to 375°F. Bake tartlet crusts until lightly golden, pressing any bubbles with back of fork, about 15 minutes. Cool crusts completely on rack.

Spread curd in crusts. Spoon blueberry topping over. (*Can be prepared ahead. Let stand at room temperature up to 2 hours or refrigerate up to 1 day.*)

8 SERVINGS

Cherry Tart

CRUST

- 2 cups all purpose flour
- ½ cup sugar
- 1 teaspoon salt
- 1 cup (2 sticks) chilled unsalted butter, cut into ½-inch cubes
- 1 large egg

FILLING

- 1 cup cherry preserves
- ½ cup chopped dried Bing (sweet) cherries
- ½ teaspoon grated lemon peel
- ¼ teaspoon almond extract
- ¼ cup unsalted natural pistachios, chopped

GLAZE

- 1 large egg
- 2 tablespoons whole milk
- 2 tablespoons sugar

FOR CRUST: Combine flour, sugar, and salt in processor; blend 5 seconds. Add butter and cut in, using on/off turns, until mixture resembles fine meal. Add egg and process just until moist clumps form. Gather into ball; divide in half. Flatten each half into disk. Wrap in plastic; chill until firm enough to roll, about 1 hour. (*Can be made 1 day ahead. Keep chilled.*)

FOR FILLING: Position rack in bottom third of oven and preheat to 325°F. Mix preserves, chopped cherries, peel, and almond extract in medium bowl. Roll out 1 dough disk on lightly floured surface to 11-inch round. Transfer round to 9-inch-diameter tart pan with removable bottom. Press dough gently into pan; trim overhang even with top of pan sides. Spread filling in crust; sprinkle with pistachios. Roll out second dough disk on lightly floured surface to 11-inch round; cut into ¾-inch-wide strips. Arrange several strips, spaced ¾ inch apart, over filling. Top with more strips at slight angle, forming lattice. Press strip ends to edge of pan, trimming overhang.

FOR GLAZE: Beat egg and milk in small bowl to blend. Brush some of glaze over lattice; sprinkle with sugar. Bake tart until crust is golden and filling is bubbling thickly, about 1 hour 5 minutes. Cool tart completely in pan on rack. (*Tart can be prepared 1 day ahead. Cover and store at room temperature.*)

8 TO 10 SERVINGS

Chocolate and Mixed-Nut Tart in Cookie Crust

CRUST

1½ cups all purpose flour

¼ cup sugar

½ cup (1 stick) plus 1 tablespoon chilled salted butter, cut into ½-inch pieces

2 tablespoons (or more) chilled whipping cream

1½ teaspoons vanilla extract

FILLING

¾ cup whole almonds (about 4½ ounces), toasted, cooled

¾ cup hazelnuts (about 4 ounces), toasted, husked, cooled

¾ cup walnuts (about 3½ ounces), toasted, cooled

¾ cup light corn syrup

¼ cup (packed) golden brown sugar

¼ cup (½ stick) salted butter, melted, cooled

3 large eggs

1 teaspoon vanilla extract

½ teaspoon almond extract

1 cup semisweet chocolate chips

FOR CRUST: Combine flour and sugar in processor. Add butter and cut in, using on/off turns, until mixture resembles coarse meal. Add 2 tablespoons cream and vanilla extract. Using on/off turns, blend until moist clumps form, adding more cream by tablespoonfuls if dough is dry. Gather dough together. Press dough over bottom and up sides of 11-inch-diameter tart pan with removable bottom. *(Can be made 1 day ahead. Cover and chill. Let stand at room temperature 30 minutes before filling.)*

FOR FILLING: Preheat oven to 350°F. Combine all nuts in processor; chop coarsely, using on/off turns. Whisk corn syrup, brown sugar, and melted butter in large bowl to blend. Whisk in eggs and vanilla and almond extracts. Mix in chocolate chips, then nuts. Transfer filling to prepared crust.

Bake tart until firmly set in center and top is deep golden, about 50 minutes. Cool in pan on rack 30 minutes. Push up pan bottom to release tart. Serve warm or at room temperature.

10 TO 12 SERVINGS

Strawberry and White Chocolate Mousse Tart

CRUST

1¼ cups unbleached all purpose flour

¼ cup sugar

¼ teaspoon salt

½ cup (1 stick) chilled unsalted butter, cut into ½-inch pieces

1 large egg yolk

1 tablespoon (or more) ice water

MOUSSE

6 ounces good-quality white chocolate, chopped

1¼ cups chilled whipping cream

½ teaspoon vanilla extract

2 large egg whites

⅛ teaspoon cream of tartar

⅓ cup seedless strawberry jam

1 tablespoon fresh lemon juice

1 16-ounce basket strawberries, hulled, thinly sliced lengthwise

FOR CRUST: Blend flour, sugar, and salt in processor. Add butter and cut in using on/off turns until mixture resembles coarse meal. Whisk egg yolk and 1 tablespoon ice water in small bowl to blend; add to processor and process until moist clumps form, adding more ice water by teaspoonfuls if dough is dry. Gather dough into ball; flatten into disk. Roll out dough on floured surface to 13-inch round. Transfer dough to 9-inch-diameter tart pan with removable bottom. Trim overhang to ¹/₂ inch. Fold overhang in and press onto sides, forming double-thick sides. Pierce crust all over with fork. Freeze crust 30 minutes.

Preheat oven to 375°F. Line crust with foil; fill with dried beans or pie weights. Bake until crust sides are light brown, about 25 minutes. Remove foil and beans; bake until crust is cooked through and golden, about 20 minutes longer. Cool crust completely in pan on rack.

FOR MOUSSE: Combine chocolate and ¹/₄ cup cream in large metal bowl. Set bowl over saucepan of simmering water (do not allow bowl to touch water) and stir until chocolate is smooth. Remove bowl from over water; cool until lukewarm, about 15 minutes.

Beat remaining 1 cup whipping cream and vanilla in large bowl until peaks form. Using clean dry beaters, beat egg whites with cream of tartar in medium bowl until stiff but not dry. Fold whites into chocolate mixture, then fold in whipped cream. Transfer mixture to cooled crust; smooth top. Chill overnight.

Combine jam and lemon juice in small saucepan; bring to simmer, stirring over medium heat until jam melts. Remove from heat. Arrange sliced strawberries in concentric circles atop tart. Brush berries with melted jam mixture. Chill tart up to 2 hours and serve.

8 SERVINGS

Apple Crostata with Cheddar Cheese

CRUST

- 1 cup all purpose flour
- 1 teaspoon sugar
- ¼ teaspoon salt
- ½ cup (1 stick) chilled unsalted butter, cut into ½-inch pieces
- 1 large egg yolk
- 1 tablespoon (or more) ice water
- ½ teaspoon vanilla extract

FILLING

- ¼ cup sugar
- ¼ teaspoon ground cinnamon
- ¼ teaspoon ground ginger
- 1½ pounds Fuji apples (about 3 large), peeled, quartered, cored, cut into ¼-inch-thick slices
- 1 tablespoon unsalted butter, cut into small pieces
- 8 ounces sharp cheddar cheese, cut into 8 wedges

FOR CRUST: Mix flour, sugar, and salt in processor. Cut in butter, using on/off turns, until mixture resembles coarse meal. Whisk yolk, 1 tablespoon ice water, and vanilla extract in small bowl to blend. Add egg mixture to processor; blend until dough clumps together, adding more ice water by teaspoonfuls if dough is dry. Form dough into ball; flatten into disk. Wrap in plastic wrap; chill at least 1 hour.

Roll out dough on floured surface to 12-inch round. Transfer to 9-inch-diameter tart pan with removable bottom. Trim dough overhang to 1 inch; fold dough overhang in and press onto sides of pan. Pierce crust all over with fork. Refrigerate crust for 1 hour.

FOR FILLING: Position rack in bottom third of oven and preheat to 400°F. Mix first 3 ingredients in bowl. Arrange apple slices in concentric circles in crust, overlapping and fitting tightly together. Sprinkle with sugar mixture. Dot with butter. Bake until apples are tender and beginning to brown and crust is golden, about 55 minutes. Cool tart in pan on rack at least 45 minutes. (*Can be made 6 hours ahead. Let stand at room temperature.*)

Serve tart slightly warm or at room temperature with cheese.

8 SERVINGS

**Harvest Dinner
for 6**

Mixed Green Salad

Braised Veal with
Aromatic Vegetables
(page 54)

French Bread

Merlot

Apple Crostata with
Cheddar Cheese
(at left)

Sweet Potato Tart with Pecans and Marshmallows

CRUST

1½ cups all purpose flour

¾ cup whole almonds

½ teaspoon salt

½ cup (1 stick) unsalted butter, room temperature

⅓ cup powdered sugar

1 large egg

FILLING

1 1-pound yam (red-skinned sweet potato)

¾ cup sugar

½ cup whipping cream

2 large eggs

1 teaspoon vanilla extract

½ teaspoon ground cinnamon

¼ teaspoon ground ginger

⅛ teaspoon ground nutmeg

⅛ teaspoon salt

1 cup mini marshmallows

½ cup pecans, toasted, chopped

Sweetened whipped cream

FOR CRUST: Blend flour, almonds, and salt in processor until almonds are finely ground. Using electric mixer, beat butter and powdered sugar in large bowl until fluffy. Add egg and beat until just blended. Add flour mixture in 2 additions, beating until moist clumps form. Gather dough into ball. Flatten into disk. Chill until firm, at least 1 hour and up to 1 day. Soften dough slightly before rolling out.

Roll out dough on lightly floured surface to 14-inch round. Transfer dough to 10-inch-diameter tart pan with removable bottom. Fold in overhang, pressing to form double-thick sides. Pierce bottom of crust all over with fork. Chill crust at least 30 minutes and up to 1 hour.

Preheat oven to 325°F. Bake crust until pale golden, about 25 minutes. Transfer to rack and cool completely. *(Can be made 1 day ahead. Store in airtight container at room temperature.)*

FOR FILLING: Preheat oven to 375°F. Roast yam on foil-lined baking sheet until very tender when pierced with skewer, about 45 minutes. Halve yam lengthwise; cool completely.

Scoop 1 cup yam pulp into blender (reserve remaining pulp for another use). Add sugar, cream, eggs, vanilla, spices, and salt and process until smooth. Sprinkle marshmallows and pecans over prepared crust. Pour batter over.

Bake tart until filling is set, about 35 minutes. Transfer to rack and cool. *(Can be made 1 day ahead. Cover; refrigerate.)* Serve cold or at room temperature with whipped cream.

12 SERVINGS

Apple-Almond Crisp

TOPPING

1½ cups all purpose flour

½ cup (packed) golden brown sugar

2 teaspoons ground cinnamon

¾ cup (1½ sticks) chilled salted butter, cut into ½-inch pieces

1 cup sliced almonds (about 4½ ounces)

FILLING

¾ cup sugar

3 tablespoons all purpose flour

1 tablespoon grated lemon peel

1½ teaspoons ground cinnamon

¾ teaspoon ground nutmeg

8 small Granny Smith apples (about 4½ pounds), peeled, halved, cored, thinly sliced

1½ teaspoons vanilla extract

¾ teaspoon almond extract

FOR TOPPING: Whisk flour, brown sugar, and cinnamon in medium bowl to blend well. Add butter and rub in with fingertips until mixture holds together in small, moist clumps. Mix in almonds; cover and chill until ready to use. (*Can be made up to 3 days ahead.*)

FOR FILLING: Preheat oven to 350°F. Butter 13x9x2-inch glass baking dish. Combine first 5 ingredients in large bowl; whisk to blend well. Mix in apples, then vanilla and almond extracts.

Spoon filling into prepared dish. Sprinkle topping over. Bake until apples are tender and topping is golden and crisp, about 1 hour. Cool at least 10 minutes; serve warm.

10 TO 12 SERVINGS

Oranges Poached in Riesling and Rosemary Syrup

1 750-ml bottle Johannisberg Riesling

⅔ cup sugar

4 navel oranges, peel and white pith removed, oranges cut crosswise in half

2 3x½-inch strips orange peel (orange part only), cut into slivers

1 teaspoon fresh whole rosemary leaves (stripped from stems)

Combine wine and sugar in heavy large saucepan. Bring to boil over medium-high heat, stirring until sugar dissolves. Reduce heat; simmer 10 minutes. Add oranges, peel, and rosemary. Simmer 8 minutes. Using slotted spoon, transfer oranges to medium bowl. Boil liquid in saucepan until reduced to 1⅓ cups, about 8 minutes. Pour syrup over oranges. Chill until cold, about 4 hours. (*Can be made 1 day ahead. Cover and keep chilled.*)

4 SERVINGS

Grilled Nectarines with Honey-Balsamic Glaze

½ cup plus 2 tablespoons honey

¼ cup balsamic vinegar

½ teaspoon vanilla extract

1 8-ounce container crème fraîche or sour cream

6 firm but ripe nectarines, halved, pitted

Whisk ½ cup honey, vinegar, and vanilla in small bowl. Whisk crème fraîche and remaining 2 tablespoons honey in medium bowl to blend. *(Glaze and crème fraîche mixture can be made 1 day ahead. Cover separately. Chill crème fraîche mixture. Rewhisk both before using.)*

Prepare barbecue (medium-high heat). Brush nectarines generously with half of glaze. Grill until heated through, turning occasionally, about 4 minutes. Arrange 2 nectarine halves, cut side up, on each plate. Drizzle with remaining glaze. Spoon some crème fraîche mixture into center of each nectarine half and serve.

6 SERVINGS

Cherry-Chocolate Shortcakes with Kirsch Whipped Cream

BISCUITS

- 2 cups all purpose flour
- ¼ cup sugar
- 1 tablespoon baking powder
- ½ teaspoon salt
- ½ cup (1 stick) chilled unsalted butter, cut into ½-inch cubes
- 3 ounces semisweet chocolate, coarsely grated
- ½ cup chilled whole milk
- 1 large egg

CHERRIES

- 1½ pounds fresh Bing cherries, stemmed, pitted, halved
- ¼ cup sugar
- 1 tablespoon kirsch (clear cherry brandy)
- ⅓ cup cherry jam

TOPPING

- 1½ cups chilled whipping cream
- 2 tablespoons sugar
- 1 tablespoon kirsch

FOR BISCUITS: Preheat oven to 400°F. Line large baking sheet with parchment paper. Combine flour, sugar, baking powder, and salt in large bowl; whisk to blend. Add butter and rub in with fingertips until mixture resembles coarse meal. Mix in chocolate. Beat milk and egg in small bowl to blend. Gradually add milk mixture to dry ingredients, tossing until dough comes together in moist clumps. Gather dough together. Turn out onto lightly floured surface and gently knead 5 turns to combine. Shape gently into 8-inch-long log. Cut log crosswise into 8 rounds; shape each into 2½x¾-inch round. Arrange rounds on prepared baking sheet.

Bake biscuits until bottoms are golden and tester inserted into center comes out clean, about 15 minutes. Cool on rack 15 minutes. (*Can be made 6 hours ahead. Cool completely. Wrap in foil and rewarm in 350°F oven 10 minutes before continuing.*)

FOR CHERRIES: Combine cherries, sugar, and kirsch in medium bowl. Let stand until sugar dissolves and juices form, tossing occasionally, about 3 hours. Strain cherry juices into heavy medium saucepan. Mix in jam. Cook over medium heat until jam melts and juices form thick syrup, stirring often, about 8 minutes. Mix syrup into cherries. (*Can be made 2 hours ahead. Let stand at room temperature.*)

FOR TOPPING: Beat cream, sugar, and kirsch in large bowl until peaks form. Cover and refrigerate up to 2 hours.

Cut biscuits horizontally in half. Place bottom halves in shallow bowls. Spoon cherry mixture and cream over. Cover with biscuit tops.

8 SERVINGS

Individual Toffee, Pecan, and Peach Crisps

FILLING
- 6 cups frozen sliced peaches (about 2½ pounds), thawed
- 3 tablespoons sugar
- 1 tablespoon fresh lime juice

TOPPING
- ¾ cup all purpose flour
- ⅓ cup (packed) golden brown sugar
- ¼ teaspoon salt
- 6 tablespoons (¾ stick) chilled unsalted butter, cut into pieces
- ¾ cup English toffee bits (such as Skor)
- ½ cup pecans, coarsely chopped

    Ice cream (optional)

FOR FILLING: Preheat oven to 350°F. Place six 1¼-cup ramekins or custard cups on large baking sheet. Mix peaches, sugar, and lime juice in large bowl to blend. Divide filling among ramekins.

FOR TOPPING: Whisk ¾ cup flour, brown sugar, and salt in large bowl to blend. Using fingertips, rub in butter until mixture holds together in clumps. Stir in toffee and pecans; sprinkle over filling.

Bake crisps until filling bubbles and topping is golden, about 40 minutes. Cool 10 minutes. Serve warm with ice cream, if desired.

MAKES 6

Figs with Honey-Yogurt Cream

FIGS

- 3 oranges
- 2 lemons
- 1 750-ml bottle red Zinfandel
- ¾ cup sugar
- ¼ cup honey
- 2 cinnamon sticks
- 10 whole cloves
- ½ teaspoon aniseed
- 12 ounces dried Calimyrna figs, stemmed, quartered (about 2 cups)

YOGURT CREAM

- 1½ cups plain whole-milk yogurt (preferably organic)
- ⅓ cup orange blossom honey
- 1½ cups chilled whipping cream
- 2 teaspoons unflavored gelatin

FOR FIGS: Using vegetable peeler, cut off peel from 2 oranges (orange part only) and from 1 lemon (yellow part only). Place peels in heavy large saucepan. Juice oranges and lemons. Add 1 cup orange juice and ¼ cup lemon juice to same pan (reserve any remaining juices for another use). Add red Zinfandel, sugar, honey, and spices and bring to boil, stirring until sugar dissolves. Add dried figs; reduce heat to medium-low and simmer until figs are tender and mixture is reduced to 3½ cups, about 1 hour. Transfer to bowl; cover and chill at least 6 hours. *(Can be prepared 3 days ahead. Keep chilled.)*

FOR YOGURT CREAM: Whisk yogurt and honey in medium bowl to blend; set aside. Place ¼ cup cream in small cup; sprinkle gelatin over. Let stand until gelatin softens and absorbs all of cream, about 15 minutes.

Bring ½ cup cream to simmer in heavy medium saucepan over medium heat. Add softened gelatin mixture and stir until gelatin dissolves completely, about 1 minute (do not boil). Remove from heat. Gradually stir in remaining ¾ cup cream. Whisk cream mixture into yogurt mixture. Divide yogurt-cream mixture among six ¾-cup custard cups or ramekins. Refrigerate yogurt creams until set, at least 4 hours. *(Can be prepared 1 day ahead. Cover and keep yogurt creams refrigerated.)*

Cut around yogurt creams to loosen. Turn out onto plates; surround with figs and syrup and serve.

6 SERVINGS

Country Bread Topped with Garden Vegetables
(page 16)

Slow-Roasted Tuna with Tomatoes, Herbs, and Spices
(page 90)

Sautéed Broccoli Rabe

Roasted Potatoes

Pinot Grigio

Figs with Honey-Yogurt Cream
(at left; pictured opposite)

Lemon Charlottes with Lemon Curd and Candied Lemon Peel

CANDIED LEMON PEEL

4 lemons

3 cups sugar

2 cups water

LEMON CURD

4 large egg yolks

2 large eggs

¾ cup sugar

½ cup fresh lemon juice

Pinch of salt

1¼ cups chilled whipping cream

42 purchased soft ladyfingers (from two 3-ounce packages)

FOR CANDIED LEMON PEEL: Line small baking sheet with foil. Using vegetable peeler, remove peel from lemons in long strips (yellow part only). Place in small saucepan. Add enough cold water to cover generously; bring to boil. Drain. Repeat blanching 2 more times. Cut lemon peel into ⅛-inch-wide strips. Bring 2 cups sugar and 2 cups water to boil in medium saucepan, stirring until sugar dissolves. Boil gently 5 minutes. Add lemon peel; simmer until peel is translucent, about 15 minutes. Using slotted spoon, transfer peel to prepared sheet; sprinkle 1 cup sugar over and toss to coat. Let dry at room temperature 2 hours. Transfer to airtight container. Pour syrup into bowl. (*Candied lemon peel and syrup can be made 3 days ahead. Store peel at room temperature. Cover and chill syrup.*)

FOR LEMON CURD: Whisk egg yolks, whole eggs, sugar, lemon juice, and salt to blend in top of double boiler over barely simmering water (do not allow bowl to touch water); whisk constantly until mixture thickens and instant-read thermometer registers 160°F, about 6 minutes. Transfer to glass bowl; place plastic directly on surface; chill overnight.

Finely chop enough candied lemon peel to measure ¼ cup; place in small bowl. Mix in ½ cup lemon curd; cover and chill. Beat whipping cream in large bowl until peaks form. Fold 1 cup whipped cream into remaining lemon curd; cover and chill. Cover remaining whipped cream; chill.

Line six ¾-cup soufflé dishes (3 inches in diameter with 1½-inch-high sides) with plastic wrap, leaving 3-inch overhang. Cut ladyfingers into 2-inch lengths, reserving ends. Stand 7 ladyfinger pieces upright side by side, rounded side out, around inside rim of each dish. Place reserved end pieces of ladyfingers in bottom of each dish, covering completely. Brush ladyfingers lightly with lemon syrup. Spoon ¼ cup lemon cream mixture into center of each dish. Gently spread generous 1 tablespoon lemon curd-peel mixture over top of each. Chill at least 2 hours. *(Can be made 1 day ahead. Cover; keep chilled.)*

Using plastic wrap as aid, lift charlottes out of soufflé dishes. Carefully peel off plastic wrap. Place on plates. Spoon reserved whipped cream into pastry bag fitted with medium star tip. Pipe whipped cream rosette atop each charlotte. Sprinkle each with candied lemon peel.

MAKES 6

Wine- and Citrus-Poached Pears with Triple-Crème Cheese

1½	cups dry red wine
⅓	cup sugar
¼	cup orange juice
1	3x¾-inch strip lemon peel (yellow part only)
1	whole clove
2	firm but ripe medium-size pears, peeled, stems left attached, halved lengthwise, cored
1	tablespoon crème de cassis (black-currant-flavored liqueur; optional)
8	ounces triple-crème cheese (such as Explorateur, Saint André, boursault, or Brillat-Savarin), cut into 4 wedges

Combine wine, sugar, orange juice, lemon peel, and clove in heavy medium saucepan. Bring to simmer over medium heat, stirring until sugar dissolves. Add pear halves to saucepan. Cut out round of parchment paper same size as saucepan. Place parchment round atop pears, pushing edges of parchment into liquid to prevent edges from curling up. Reduce heat and barely simmer until pears are tender when pierced with knife, about 12 minutes.

Using slotted spoon, transfer pears to bowl. Boil liquid in saucepan until slightly syrupy and reduced to ¾ cup, about 14 minutes. Cool to room temperature; stir in crème de cassis, if desired. Pour syrup over pears. Cover; chill at least 12 hours, turning pears occasionally.

Thinly slice pear halves lengthwise almost to stem end, leaving stems attached. Spoon generous 1 tablespoon pear syrup onto each of 4 plates. Top each with 1 pear half, pressing gently to fan. Serve with cheese.

4 SERVINGS

Spiced Plum Pavlovas

PLUMS

1½ pounds plums, halved, pitted, sliced ¼ inch thick
½ cup sugar
1 tablespoon fresh lemon juice
½ teaspoon ground cardamom

MERINGUES

4 large egg whites
¼ teaspoon cream of tartar
1 cup sugar
2 teaspoons cornstarch
½ teaspoon apple cider vinegar
½ teaspoon vanilla extract
¼ teaspoon ground cardamom

TOPPING

1½ cups chilled crème fraîche*
2 tablespoons sugar

FOR PLUMS: Combine all ingredients in large skillet; toss to coat. Cover and cook over medium-high heat until sugar dissolves, stirring occasionally, about 5 minutes. Uncover and cook until plums are tender but still hold shape, stirring occasionally, about 3 minutes longer; cool to room temperature. (*Can be made 1 day ahead. Transfer to bowl. Cover and chill.*)

FOR MERINGUES: Preheat oven to 350°F. Line large baking sheet with parchment paper. Using electric mixer, beat egg whites in large bowl 1 minute. Add cream of tartar. Continue to beat until soft peaks form. Gradually add sugar, beating until whites are thick and resemble marshmallow creme, about 5 minutes. Beat in cornstarch, vinegar, vanilla, and cardamom. Drop meringue onto prepared sheet in 6 mounds, spaced 3 inches apart. Using back of spoon, make depression in center of each.

Place meringues in oven. Immediately reduce temperature to 250°F. Bake until meringues are dry outside (but centers remain soft) and pale straw color and lift easily from parchment, about 50 minutes. Cool on sheet on rack. (*Can be made 8 hours ahead. Let stand at room temperature.*)

FOR TOPPING: Beat crème fraîche and sugar in medium bowl until peaks form. Refrigerate up to 2 hours. Place meringues on plates. Spoon plum mixture into center depression. Spoon topping and any plum juices over.

Sold at some supermarkets. If unavailable, heat 1½ cups whipping cream to lukewarm (85°F). Remove from heat and mix in 3 tablespoons buttermilk. Cover and let stand in warm draft-free area until slightly thickened, 24 to 48 hours. Refrigerate until ready to use.

6 SERVINGS

Individual Ginger Cakes with Apricot Sticky Sauce

SAUCE

2/3 cup dried apricots, thinly sliced

3 tablespoons chopped crystallized ginger

1 cup sugar

3 tablespoons water

1 tablespoon light corn syrup

1 tablespoon salted butter

2/3 cup whipping cream

1 teaspoon vanilla extract

CAKES

Nonstick vegetable oil spray

2½ cups all purpose flour

4 teaspoons ground ginger

2 teaspoons baking soda

1½ teaspoons ground allspice

1 cup hot water

1 tablespoon instant espresso powder

1 cup (packed) golden brown sugar

¾ cup (1½ sticks) salted butter, room temperature

1 cup mild-flavored (light) molasses

2 large eggs

2 tablespoons finely grated peeled fresh ginger

2 teaspoons sugar

FOR SAUCE: Combine apricots and ginger in small bowl. Pour enough boiling water over just to cover; let soften 10 minutes. Drain; pat dry with paper towels. Combine sugar, water, and corn syrup in heavy medium skillet. Stir over low heat until sugar dissolves. Increase heat; boil until syrup is deep amber color, brushing down sides with wet pastry brush and swirling pan occasionally, about 10 minutes. Remove from heat. Mix in butter, apricots, and ginger. Add cream and vanilla. Stir over low heat until caramel bits dissolve and sauce is smooth. (*Can be made 1 day ahead. Cover; chill. Rewarm over low heat before serving.*)

FOR CAKES: Preheat oven to 350°F. Spray 9 mini-Bundt molds with nonstick spray; generously butter molds. Sift flour and next 3 ingredients into medium bowl. Combine hot water and espresso powder in small bowl and stir to dissolve. Using electric mixer, beat brown sugar and butter in large bowl until blended. Beat in molasses, then eggs and fresh ginger. Beat in flour mixture in 3 additions alternately with espresso mixture in 2 additions. Divide among molds. Sprinkle with sugar. Bake cakes until tester inserted near center comes out clean, about 20 minutes. Cool cakes 10 minutes; turn out onto baking sheet. (*Can be made 6 hours ahead; let stand at room temperature. Rewarm in 350°F oven 8 minutes.*) Serve with warm sauce.

MAKES 9

Cappuccino-Fudge Cheesecake

CRUST

- 1   9-ounce box chocolate wafer cookies
- 6   ounces bittersweet (not unsweetened) or semisweet chocolate, coarsely chopped
- ½   cup (packed) dark brown sugar
- ⅛   teaspoon ground nutmeg
- 7   tablespoons hot melted unsalted butter

Finely grind cookies, chopped chocolate, brown sugar, and nutmeg in processor. Add butter and process until crumbs begin to stick together, scraping down bowl occasionally, about 1 minute. Transfer crumbs to 10-inch-diameter springform pan with 3-inch-high sides. Wrap plastic wrap around fingers and press crumb mixture firmly up sides to within ½ inch of top edge, then over bottom of pan (**step 1**).

GANACHE

- 1½   cups whipping cream
- 20   ounces bittersweet (not unsweetened) or semisweet chocolate, chopped
- ¼   cup Kahlúa or other coffee-flavored liqueur

Bring cream to simmer in large saucepan. Remove from heat; add chocolate and Kahlúa. Whisk until chocolate is melted and ganache is smooth. Pour 2 cups ganache over bottom of crust (**step 2**). Freeze until ganache layer is firm, about 30 minutes. Reserve remaining ganache; cover and let stand at room temperature to use later for creating lattice pattern.

FILLING

- 4   8-ounce packages cream cheese, room temperature
- 1⅓   cups sugar
- 2   tablespoons all purpose flour
- 2   tablespoons dark rum
- 2   tablespoons instant espresso powder or coffee crystals
- 2   tablespoons ground whole espresso coffee beans (medium-coarse grind)
- 1   tablespoon vanilla extract
- 2   teaspoons mild-flavored (light) molasses
- 4   large eggs

Position rack in middle of oven and preheat to 350°F. Using electric mixer, beat cream cheese and sugar in large bowl until blended. Beat in flour. Stir rum, espresso powder, ground coffee, vanilla, and molasses in small bowl until instant coffee dissolves; beat into cream cheese mixture. Beat in eggs 1 at a time, occasionally scraping down sides of bowl.

Pour filling over cold ganache in crust. Place cheesecake on rimmed baking sheet. Bake until top is brown, puffed, and cracked at edges, and center 2 inches moves only slightly when pan is gently shaken, about 1 hour 5 minutes (**step 3**). Transfer to rack. Cool 15 minutes while preparing topping (top of cheesecake will fall slightly). Maintain oven temperature.

TOPPING

1½ cups sour cream

⅓ cup sugar

2 teaspoons vanilla extract

Espresso coffee beans (optional)

Whisk sour cream, sugar, and vanilla in medium bowl to blend. Pour topping over hot cheesecake, spreading to cover filling completely. Bake until topping is set, about 10 minutes. Transfer cheesecake to rack. Refrigerate hot cheesecake on rack until cool, about 3 hours.

Run small sharp knife between crust and pan sides to loosen cake; release pan sides. Transfer cheesecake to platter. Spoon reserved ganache into pastry bag fitted with small star tip. Pipe 6 diagonal lines atop cheesecake, spacing 1 inch apart. Repeat in opposite direction, making lattice (**step 4**). Pipe rosettes of ganache around top edge of cake. Garnish with coffee beans, if desired. Chill until lattice is firm, at least 6 hours. (*Can be made 4 days ahead. Wrap loosely in foil, forming dome over lattice; keep chilled.*)

12 SERVINGS

Step 1. To prevent the moist crust mixture from sticking to your fingers, cover them with plastic wrap before pressing the crust mixture into the pan.

Step 2. Pour part of the rich ganache into the prepared crust to make the fudgy layer under the filling.

Step 3. After the filling is added, bake the cheesecake until it is golden brown on top, puffed, and beginning to crack at the edges, and just set in the center.

Step 4. Create the lattice design by piping the reserved ganache in 6 evenly spaced lines in one direction. Then pipe more lines across the first lines at an angle.

Raspberry Cake with Marsala, Crème Fraîche, and Raspberries

1½ cups all purpose flour

1 teaspoon baking powder

1 teaspoon salt

¼ teaspoon baking soda

¼ teaspoon ground nutmeg

½ cup Marsala

¼ cup fresh orange juice

14 tablespoons (1¾ sticks) unsalted butter, room temperature

1 cup plus 4 tablespoons sugar

2 large eggs

1 teaspoon vanilla extract

1 teaspoon grated lemon peel

4 cups fresh raspberries

2 cups crème fraîche or sour cream

Position rack in center of oven and preheat to 400°F. Butter 10-inch-diameter springform pan. Whisk first 5 ingredients in medium bowl to blend. Combine Marsala and orange juice in small bowl. Beat 12 tablespoons butter and 1 cup sugar in large bowl until well blended. Beat in eggs, vanilla, and lemon peel. Beat in Marsala mixture in 2 additions alternately with flour mixture in 3 additions. Transfer batter to prepared pan. Sprinkle with 1 1/2 cups raspberries.

Bake cake until top is gently set, about 20 minutes. Reduce oven temperature to 375°F. Dot top of cake with 2 tablespoons butter and sprinkle with 2 tablespoons sugar. Continue baking until tester inserted into center of cake comes out clean, about 15 minutes. Cool in pan on rack. Release pan sides; transfer cake to platter. Cool to room temperature.

Mix crème fraîche and 2 tablespoons sugar in small bowl. *(Cake and crème fraîche mixture can be made 8 hours ahead. Let cake stand at room temperature. Cover and chill crème fraîche mixture.)* Cut cake into wedges. Top each with dollop of crème fraîche and fresh raspberries.

10 SERVINGS

Country Pear Cake

- 2 large eggs
- 1/3 cup olive oil (do not use extra-virgin)
- 1/4 cup whole milk
- 1 tablespoon grated lemon peel
- 2/3 cup plus 1 tablespoon sugar
- 1 1/2 cups self-rising flour
- 4 Bartlett pears (1 3/4 pounds), peeled, quartered, cored, cut crosswise into 1/4-inch-thick slices (about 3 cups)

  Powdered sugar

Preheat oven to 375°F. Oil and flour 9-inch-diameter cake pan with 1 1/2-inch-high sides. Line bottom with parchment paper. Whisk eggs, oil, milk, and lemon peel in large bowl. Whisk in 2/3 cup sugar. Add flour; whisk until batter is smooth. Mix in pears. Transfer batter to pan. Sprinkle top with 1 tablespoon sugar. Bake until brown on top and tester inserted into center comes out clean, about 40 minutes. Cool in pan on rack. *(Can be made 8 hours ahead. Let stand at room temperature.)*

Using sharp knife, cut around edge of cake to loosen. Turn cake out onto rack. Invert onto platter right-side up. Sift powdered sugar over top.

6 SERVINGS

Dinner and a Movie for 6

Romaine Salad with Chives and Blue Cheese
(page 146)

Mahogany Beef Stew with Red Wine Sauce
(page 53)

Mashed Potatoes

Cabernet Sauvignon

Country Pear Cake
(at left)

Sour Cream Layer Cake with Pecan Brittle

PECAN BRITTLE

  Nonstick vegetable oil spray

¾ cup sugar

¼ cup water

⅛ teaspoon cream of tartar

¾ cup pecan halves, toasted, coarsely chopped

CAKE

  Nonstick vegetable oil spray

1 18.25-ounce box yellow cake mix

4 large eggs

1 cup sour cream

⅓ cup vegetable oil

½ teaspoon vanilla extract

½ teaspoon almond extract

2 ounces bittersweet (not unsweetened) or semisweet chocolate, coarsely grated

FROSTING

½ cup (packed) dark brown sugar

3 tablespoons water

¼ cup whipping cream

6 cups (about) powdered sugar

1 cup (2 sticks) unsalted butter, room temperature

FOR PECAN BRITTLE: Spray baking sheet with nonstick spray. Combine sugar, ¼ cup water, and cream of tartar in heavy small saucepan. Stir over medium-low heat until sugar dissolves. Increase heat and boil without stirring until syrup is deep amber color, occasionally brushing down sides of pan with wet pastry brush, about 9 minutes. Add chopped pecans and swirl to blend. Pour out onto prepared baking sheet; spread evenly. Cool brittle completely. Cut 3 large pieces of brittle (each about 1½ inches). Cut remaining brittle into ⅓-inch pieces. (*Can be made 1 week ahead. Store airtight at room temperature.*)

FOR CAKE: Preheat oven to 350°F. Spray two 9-inch-diameter cake pans with 1½-inch-high sides with nonstick spray. Line bottom of pans with waxed paper. Combine cake mix, eggs, sour cream, oil, vanilla extract, and almond extract in large bowl. Using electric mixer, beat mixture until well blended, about 3 minutes; fold in grated bittersweet chocolate. Divide batter equally between prepared pans.

Bake cakes until brown on top and tester inserted into center comes out clean, about 30 minutes. Cool cakes in pans on racks 10 minutes. Cut around cakes to loosen; turn out onto racks. Peel off paper and cool cakes completely.

FOR FROSTING: Combine ½ cup brown sugar and 3 tablespoons water in heavy small saucepan. Stir over medium-low heat until sugar dissolves. Increase heat; boil until slightly thickened, about 3 minutes. Remove from heat; cool 5 minutes. Mix in cream. Beat 3 cups powdered sugar and butter in large bowl until well blended. Beat in brown sugar mixture. Beat in enough remaining powdered sugar to form frosting that is thick enough to spread.

Place 1 cake layer, flat side up, on platter. Spread with 1 cup frosting. Sprinkle with ½ cup small brittle pieces; press into frosting. Top with second cake layer, flat side down. Spread remaining frosting over top and sides of cake. Stand large brittle pieces in center of cake. Arrange smaller brittle pieces in 1-inch-wide border around top edge of cake. (*Can be made 1 day ahead. Cover with cake dome and refrigerate. Let stand at room temperature 1 hour before serving.*)

10 TO 12 SERVINGS

Cinnamon-Sugar Plum Cake

1¼	cups all purpose flour
1	teaspoon baking powder
¼	teaspoon salt
½	cup (1 stick) unsalted butter, room temperature
¾	cup plus 1½ tablespoons sugar
2	large eggs
1	tablespoon fresh lemon juice
1	teaspoon grated lemon peel
5	large plums (about 1¼ pounds), pitted, cut into ½-inch wedges
¼	teaspoon ground cinnamon

Preheat oven to 350°F. Butter 9-inch-diameter springform pan. Whisk first 3 ingredients in small bowl to blend. Using electric mixer, beat butter in large bowl until fluffy. Beat in ¾ cup sugar. Add eggs 1 at a time, then lemon juice and lemon peel, beating until blended after each addition. Beat in flour mixture. Spread batter in prepared pan.

Press plum wedges halfway into batter in concentric circles, spacing slightly apart. Mix remaining 1½ tablespoons sugar and cinnamon in small bowl; sprinkle over plums.

Bake until cake is browned on top and tester inserted into center comes out clean, about 50 minutes. Cut around cake; release pan sides. Serve cake warm or at room temperature.

6 TO 8 SERVINGS

Chocolate-Espresso Lava Cakes with Espresso Whipped Cream

        1   cup all purpose flour
      ¾   cup unsweetened cocoa powder
        6   teaspoons instant espresso powder or instant coffee powder
    1½   teaspoons baking powder
        1   cup (2 sticks) salted butter, melted
        1   cup sugar
        1   cup (packed) golden brown sugar
        4   large eggs
    1½   teaspoons vanilla extract
      ¼   teaspoon almond extract
      12   tablespoons semisweet chocolate chips (about 4½ ounces)

        1   cup chilled whipping cream
        3   tablespoons powdered sugar

Sift flour, cocoa powder, 5 teaspoons espresso powder, and baking powder into medium bowl. Place butter in large bowl; add both sugars and whisk until well blended. Whisk in eggs 1 at a time, then vanilla and almond extracts. Whisk in dry ingredients. Divide batter among six 1-cup ovenproof coffee mugs (about ⅔ cup in each). Top each with 2 tablespoons chocolate chips. Gently press chips into batter. Cover and refrigerate mugs at least 1 hour and up to 1 day.

Combine cream, powdered sugar, and 1 teaspoon espresso powder in medium bowl; whisk until peaks form. Chill up to 1 hour.

Position rack in center of oven and preheat to 350°F. Let mugs with batter stand at room temperature 5 minutes. Bake uncovered until cakes are puffed and crusty and tester inserted into center comes out with thick batter attached, about 30 minutes. Cool cakes 5 minutes. Top hot cakes with espresso whipped cream and serve.

6 SERVINGS

Dinner in the Kitchen for 6

Spinach Salad with Oranges and Almonds
(page 146)

Farfalle and Tuna Casserole
(page 124)

Sauvignon Blanc

Chocolate-Espresso Lava Cakes with Espresso Whipped Cream
(at left; pictured opposite)

Mixed-Berry Chiffon Cake with Almond Cream Cheese Frosting

ALMOND CREAM FILLING

- 1 cup half and half
- 1 vanilla bean, split lengthwise
- ⅓ cup sugar
- ¼ cup all purpose flour
- 2 large eggs
- ½ 7-ounce roll almond paste (scant ½ cup packed), diced
- 6 ounces good-quality white chocolate (such as Lindt or Baker's), finely chopped
- 2 tablespoons (¼ stick) unsalted butter
- ⅔ cup chilled heavy whipping cream

Pour half and half into medium saucepan. Scrape in seeds from vanilla bean; add bean and bring to simmer. Remove from heat; cover and steep 15 minutes. Blend sugar and flour in medium bowl. Whisk in eggs, then warm half and half mixture; return to same pan. Add almond paste. Whisk over medium heat until almond paste dissolves and custard boils, about 10 minutes. Remove from heat. Add white chocolate and butter; whisk until smooth. Press plastic onto custard; chill 3 hours. Remove vanilla bean. Beat cream to peaks; fold into custard in 3 additions. Cover; chill at least 6 hours. *(Can be made 2 days ahead. Keep chilled.)*

CAKE

- 1½ cups cake flour
- 1¼ cups sugar
- 1 tablespoon baking powder
- ½ teaspoon salt
- ½ cup lukewarm water
- ½ cup vegetable oil
- 5 large eggs, separated
- 1 tablespoon vanilla extract
- ½ teaspoon almond extract
- 2 teaspoons grated lemon peel
- 1 cup raspberry preserves

Preheat oven to 325°F. Butter and flour two 10-inch-diameter cake pans with 2-inch-high sides. Sift flour, ¾ cup sugar, baking powder, and salt into large bowl. Using electric mixer, beat ½ cup lukewarm water into dry ingredients; beat in oil, egg yolks, both extracts, and peel. Using clean dry beaters, beat whites in medium bowl until soft peaks form. Gradually add remaining ½ cup sugar, beating until stiff but not dry. Fold whites into batter in 3 additions. Measure 4⅔ cups batter into 1 prepared pan and 3⅓ cups batter into second pan. Bake cakes until tester inserted into center comes out clean, about 25 minutes for thinner cake and 30 minutes for larger cake. Cool cakes in pans on racks 10 minutes. Cut around

Step 1. Drop dollops of almond cream filling (instead of one large mass) onto the cake to make the filling easier to spread.

Step 2. Use the bottom of a tart pan to help transfer the delicate cake layers from the rack to the cake during assembly.

cakes and turn out onto racks; cool. Place thinner cake on 9-inch-diameter tart pan bottom. Spread with ¹/₂ cup preserves, leaving ¹/₂-inch plain border. Spoon 1¹/₂ cups filling in dollops atop preserves; spread evenly (**step 1**). Chill until filling is firm, 15 minutes. Cut larger cake horizontally in half. Place 1 half, cut side down, atop chilled filling. Spread with ¹/₂ cup preserves, leaving ¹/₂-inch plain border. Spoon 1¹/₂ cups filling atop preserves; spread evenly. Top with remaining cake layer, cut side down (**step 2**). Cover cake and remaining filling; chill 3 hours.

Step 3. Spread an initial thin coating of frosting (called a crumb coat) over the cake to provide a smooth, crumb-free surface for the final decorative layer of frosting.

ALMOND CREAM CHEESE FROSTING

2¹/₂ 8-ounce packages cream cheese, room temperature
¹/₂ cup (1 stick) unsalted butter, room temperature
1¹/₂ cups powdered sugar
1 tablespoon vanilla extract
³/₄ teaspoon almond extract

Assorted fresh berries (such as strawberries and blueberries)
Currant jelly, warmed

Beat first 5 ingredients in large bowl to blend. Beat in ³/₄ cup remaining filling. Spread 1 cup frosting thinly over sides and top of cake (**step 3**). Spread cake with remaining frosting, building high rim around top edge (**step 4**). *(Can be made 1 day ahead. Cover with cake dome and chill.)*

Mound berries on top of cake. Brush top of berries with warm jelly to glaze. Serve immediately, or chill up to 6 hours.

14 SERVINGS

Step 4. Build up a rim of frosting along the top edge of the cake to hold the fresh-fruit topping in place.

Chocolate Almond Torte

1½ cups blanched slivered almonds

1 cup sugar

8 ounces bittersweet (not unsweetened) or semisweet chocolate, chopped

5 large eggs, separated

½ teaspoon almond extract

½ teaspoon grated lemon peel

½ cup (1 stick) unsalted butter, melted, cooled

¼ teaspoon salt

Powdered sugar

Preheat oven to 350°F. Butter 10-inch-diameter springform pan with 2¾-inch-high sides. Combine almonds and ⅓ cup sugar in processor. Blend until almonds are very finely ground. Transfer almond mixture to medium bowl; do not clean processor. Add chocolate and ⅓ cup sugar to processor. Blend until chocolate is finely ground but not beginning to clump, about 45 seconds; stir into almond mixture. Using electric mixer, beat yolks and ⅓ cup sugar in large bowl until mixture falls in heavy ribbon when beaters are lifted, about 5 minutes. Beat in almond extract and lemon peel. Fold in chocolate-almond mixture, then butter.

Using clean dry beaters, beat egg whites and salt in another large bowl until stiff but not

dry. Fold beaten egg whites into chocolate batter in 3 additions. Transfer batter to prepared pan.

Bake cake until tester inserted into center comes out with moist crumbs attached, about 40 minutes. Cool cake completely in pan on rack. *(Can be made 1 day ahead. Cover; store at room temperature.)* Cut around pan sides to loosen; release sides. Sift powdered sugar over cake.

12 SERVINGS

Cherry-Vanilla Tea Cake with Vanilla Sugar

1½ cups all purpose flour
1 teaspoon baking powder
½ teaspoon baking soda
¼ teaspoon salt
⅛ teaspoon ground nutmeg
½ cup (1 stick) unsalted butter, room temperature
1 cup plus 1 tablespoon sugar
2 large eggs, room temperature
2 teaspoons vanilla extract
⅔ cup sour cream
1 teaspoon grated lemon peel
1 cup canned pitted sweet cherries, halved, drained

½ vanilla bean, split lengthwise
2 tablespoons powdered sugar

Preheat oven to 350°F. Lightly butter and flour 10-inch springform pan. Sift first 5 ingredients into medium bowl. Using electric mixer, beat butter and 1 cup sugar in large bowl until well blended. Add eggs 1 at a time, beating well after each addition. Blend in vanilla. Transfer 2 tablespoons dry ingredients to small bowl. On low speed, beat half of remaining dry ingredients into butter mixture, then mix in sour cream and lemon peel. Beat in remaining half of dry ingredients. Mix cherries into reserved 2 tablespoons dry ingredients; fold cherries into batter.

Spoon batter into prepared pan; smooth top with spoon. Bake until tester inserted into center of cake comes out clean, about 30 minutes. Transfer cake to rack and cool 10 minutes.

Meanwhile, using small sharp knife, scrape seeds from vanilla bean into small bowl. Mix in 1 tablespoon sugar, rubbing with fingertips to distribute seeds. Add powdered sugar and rub again.

Sift vanilla sugar over hot cake and cool. Cut around pan sides to loosen cake; remove pan sides. (*Can be made 1 day ahead. Cover; let stand at room temperature.*)

10 SERVINGS

Housewarming Party for 10

Stuffed Crimini Mushrooms
(*page 19*)

Caesar Salad

Pacific Coast Bouillabaisse
(*page 96*)

Crusty Bread

Pinot Grigio

Chocolate Almond Torte
(*opposite*)

Phyllo Cups with Chocolate Mousse and Fresh Fruit

PHYLLO CUPS

9 fresh phyllo pastry sheets or frozen, thawed (each about 17x13 inches), stacked and halved crosswise, forming eighteen 8½x13-inch rectangles

10 tablespoons (1¼ sticks) unsalted butter, melted

8 tablespoons (about) sugar

8 tablespoons (about) finely chopped toasted hazelnuts

CHOCOLATE MOUSSE

4 large eggs, separated

½ cup sugar

¼ cup (½ stick) unsalted butter, cut into ½-inch pieces

¼ cup water

1 teaspoon instant espresso powder

8 ounces bittersweet (not unsweetened) or semisweet chocolate, chopped

1 ½-pint basket fresh raspberries

2 ripe pears, peeled, diced

FOR PHYLLO CUPS: Preheat oven to 375°F. Generously butter every other cup in 12-cup muffin pan. Place 1 phyllo rectangle on work surface; cover remaining phyllo with plastic wrap and damp cloth to prevent drying. Brush rectangle with melted butter; sprinkle with ½ tablespoon sugar and ½ tablespoon hazelnuts. Place second phyllo rectangle atop first; brush with butter and sprinkle with ½ tablespoon sugar and ½ tablespoon hazelnuts. Repeat 3 more times; top with 1 more rectangle and brush with butter, making stack of 6 rectangles. Using small sharp knife and 6-inch-diameter plate as guide, cut out two 6-inch round stacks. Press each stack into 1 buttered muffin cup. Repeat procedure 2 more times, making 4 more phyllo cups (6 total). Bake phyllo cups until golden and crisp, about 10 minutes. Immediately lift phyllo cups from pan, twisting carefully to loosen; place on rack. Cool completely. (*Can be made 2 days ahead. Store airtight at room temperature.*)

FOR MOUSSE: Whisk egg yolks, ¼ cup sugar, butter, ¼ cup water, and espresso powder in large metal bowl to blend. Set bowl over saucepan of simmering water (do not let bowl touch water); whisk constantly until thermometer inserted into mixture registers 160°F, about 3 minutes. Add chocolate; whisk until smooth. Turn off heat; leave bowl over water.

Using electric mixer, beat egg whites in another large bowl to soft peaks. Gradually add remaining ¼ cup sugar, beating until stiff and glossy. Remove chocolate from over water. Fold ⅓ of beaten whites into warm chocolate mixture to lighten. Fold in remaining whites. Cover and chill until set, at least 3 hours or overnight.

Fill phyllo cups with mousse (reserve remaining mousse for another use). Top with raspberries and diced pears and serve.

6 SERVINGS

MOUSSES &
PUDDINGS

Pineapple and Banana Couscous Pudding

¾ cup water

½ cup plain couscous

1 tablespoon unsalted butter

½ large banana, chopped (about ½ cup)

1 tablespoon (packed) golden brown sugar

1½ cups plus 2 tablespoons chilled whipping cream

5 tablespoons sweetened cream of coconut (such as Coco López)*

1 tablespoon triple sec

½ cup candied pineapple, minced

1½ cups diced peeled fresh pineapple

Bring ¾ cup water to boil in heavy medium saucepan over high heat. Stir in couscous. Remove from heat. Cover and let stand until water is absorbed, about 15 minutes. Fluff couscous with fork.

Melt butter in small nonstick skillet over medium-high heat. Add chopped banana and brown sugar and sauté until banana is soft, about 1 minute. Cool.

Using electric mixer, beat cream in large bowl until soft peaks form. Fold in cream of coconut and triple sec. Reserve 6 tablespoons whipped cream mixture for topping. Fold candied pineapple, couscous, and banana into remaining whipped cream mixture in large bowl. Divide among 6 parfait glasses or dessert bowls. (*Can be made 4 hours ahead. Cover whipped cream mixture and puddings separately; chill.*)

Top each pudding with some of reserved whipped cream mixture. Sprinkle each with fresh pineapple and serve.

Cream of coconut is available in the liquor section of most supermarkets.

6 SERVINGS

Moscato Zabaglione with Cornmeal Cookies

COOKIES

- ½ cup (1 stick) unsalted butter, room temperature
- ½ cup sugar
- 1 teaspoon grated lemon peel
- ½ teaspoon salt
- 2 large egg yolks
- ½ cup yellow cornmeal
- 1¼ cups all purpose flour
- ⅔ cup golden raisins (about 4 ounces)

    Powdered sugar

ZABAGLIONE

- 6 large egg yolks
- ⅓ cup sugar
- ¾ cup Italian Moscato or Essencia

FOR COOKIES: Using electric mixer, beat butter and ¹/₂ cup sugar in large bowl until fluffy. Beat in lemon peel and salt, then egg yolks. Beat in cornmeal, then flour. Stir in raisins. Knead dough just to combine; transfer to sheet of plastic wrap. Using plastic, form dough into 2x9-inch log. Refrigerate until firm, 3 hours or up to 1 day.

Preheat oven to 325°F. Line large baking sheet with parchment paper. Slice dough log into ¹/₄-inch-thick rounds. Arrange rounds on prepared baking sheet, spacing 1 inch apart and reshaping into rounds if uneven. Bake cookies until golden at edges, about 15 minutes. Transfer to rack. Dust with powdered sugar and cool completely. (*Can be made 3 days ahead. Store in airtight container at room temperature.*)

FOR ZABAGLIONE: Whisk egg yolks and sugar in large metal bowl to blend; gradually whisk in Moscato. Set bowl over saucepan of simmering water (do not allow bowl to touch water). Whisk until mixture is thick and foamy and thermometer inserted into mixture registers 160°F, about 4 minutes. Divide zabaglione among 6 wineglasses. Serve immediately, passing cookies alongside.

6 SERVINGS

Burnt-Sugar Brûlée

½ cup plus 6 teaspoons sugar
1 tablespoon water
2 cups whipping cream

5 large egg yolks
1½ teaspoons vanilla extract
¼ teaspoon salt

Preheat oven to 300°F. Place six ½-cup ramekins or soufflé dishes in 13x9x2-inch metal baking pan. Combine ½ cup sugar and 1 tablespoon water in heavy medium saucepan. Stir over medium-low heat until sugar dissolves. Increase heat and boil without stirring until syrup is deep amber color and just begins to smell slightly burnt, occasionally brushing down sides of pan with wet pastry brush and swirling pan, about 5 minutes. Slowly add cream (mixture will bubble vigorously); stir over low heat until any caramel bits dissolve and mixture is smooth. Remove from heat. Cool slightly.

Combine egg yolks, vanilla, and salt in medium metal bowl. Using electric mixer, beat until mixture is pale in color, about 3 minutes. Gradually add cream mixture and beat until blended. Divide mixture among ramekins (ramekins will not be full). Pour enough hot water into baking pan to come halfway up sides of ramekins. Bake until custards are just set, about 45 minutes. Remove ramekins from pan; cool slightly. Chill until cold, then cover with plastic; chill overnight.

Preheat broiler. Place ramekins on baking sheet. Sprinkle each custard with 1 teaspoon sugar. Broil until sugar melts and is golden brown, turning baking sheet as necessary and watching closely to avoid burning, about 3 minutes. Chill 30 minutes to 2 hours.

MAKES 6

Bread Pudding with Currants and Caramel

SAUCE

- 1 pound dark brown sugar
- 2 cups whipping cream
- 1 cup light corn syrup
- ½ cup dark rum

PUDDING

- 2½ cups whole milk
- 1 cup whipping cream
- 1 cup sugar
- 4 large eggs
- 4 large egg yolks
- 1 tablespoon vanilla extract
- ¼ teaspoon ground nutmeg
- ⅛ teaspoon salt
- 12 slices good-quality white bread, crusts trimmed
- 3 tablespoons unsalted butter, room temperature
- ½ cup dried currants

FOR SAUCE: Whisk all ingredients in heavy large saucepan to blend. Whisk over medium-high heat until beginning to boil. Reduce heat to medium-low. Simmer until sauce is thick enough to coat spoon, whisking occasionally, about 25 minutes. (*Can be made 3 days ahead. Cool. Cover and refrigerate. Rewarm over low heat before serving.*)

FOR PUDDING: Preheat oven to 350°F. Butter 11x7-inch glass baking dish. Combine milk and next 7 ingredients in large bowl; whisk to blend well. Spread 1 side of each bread slice with butter. Arrange 6 slices, buttered side up, in single layer in prepared baking dish, trimming to fit. Sprinkle with currants. Top with remaining bread slices, buttered side up. Pour custard through sieve over bread in baking dish. Let stand 15 minutes, occasionally pressing bread into custard.

Place pudding in dish in 13x9x2-inch metal baking pan. Pour enough hot water into pan to come halfway up sides of pudding dish. Place in oven. Bake pudding until set in center and golden on top, about 45 minutes. Remove pudding from water bath. Serve warm or at room temperature with warm caramel sauce.

6 TO 8 SERVINGS

Vanilla Panna Cotta with Mixed-Berry Compote

¼   cup cold water
2½ teaspoons unflavored gelatin (from 2 packages)

3   cups whipping cream
1   cup sugar
1½ teaspoons vanilla extract

4   ½-pint baskets assorted fresh berries (such as raspberries, blueberries, blackberries, and strawberries)
⅓   cup sweet white wine (such as Moscato)

Pour ¼ cup cold water into small custard cup. Sprinkle gelatin over. Let stand until gelatin softens, about 15 minutes. Bring 1 inch of water in small skillet to boil. Place cup with gelatin in water. Stir until gelatin dissolves, about 2 minutes. Remove from heat.

Combine cream and ⅔ cup sugar in heavy medium saucepan. Stir over medium heat just until sugar dissolves. Remove from heat. Mix in vanilla and gelatin. Divide pudding mixture among 8 wineglasses. Cover and chill until set, at least 6 hours and up to 1 day.

Combine berries and remaining $1/3$ cup sugar in medium bowl. Crush berries slightly with back of spoon. Mix in wine. Let compote stand until berry juices and sugar form syrup, stirring often, at least 1 hour and up to 2 hours.

Spoon compote over puddings.

8 SERVINGS

Chestnut Soufflé

2	cups whole milk
1	vanilla bean, split lengthwise
¾	cup canned sweetened chestnut spread or puree*
¼	cup plus 2 tablespoons sugar
4	large egg yolks
¼	cup (½ stick) unsalted butter
½	cup all purpose flour
2	tablespoons brandy
¼	teaspoon salt
½	cup chopped vacuum-packed chestnuts**
5	large egg whites, room temperature

Place milk in heavy small saucepan. Scrape in seeds from vanilla bean. Bring to simmer. Remove from heat. Whisk chestnut puree, $1/4$ cup sugar, and egg yolks in medium bowl; set aside.

Melt butter in heavy medium saucepan over medium heat. Add flour; stir 1 minute. Add milk mixture; whisk until mixture boils and thickens, about 8 minutes. Stir into chestnut mixture. Whisk in brandy and salt. Mix in chopped chestnuts. Cool 10 minutes.

Preheat oven to 375°F. Butter and sugar two 4-cup soufflé dishes. Using electric mixer, beat egg whites in medium bowl until soft peaks form. Beat in 2 tablespoons sugar. Continue beating until stiff but not dry. Fold $1/3$ of whites into warm soufflé base. Fold in remaining whites. Divide batter between prepared dishes.

Bake soufflés until puffed and just beginning to brown, about 30 minutes. Spoon onto plates; serve immediately.

Known as crème de marrons; available at specialty foods stores and some supermarkets across the country.
**Vacuum-packed chestnuts are sold at specialty foods stores and in the specialty foods section of some supermarkets.*

MAKES 2 SOUFFLÉS; 8 SERVINGS

Flans with Marsala and Caramel Sauce

    2 cups whipping cream
    ¾ cup sugar
    5 tablespoons sweet Marsala
    1 teaspoon grated lemon peel
    3 large eggs
    2 large egg yolks
    1 teaspoon vanilla extract

    1 cup purchased caramel sauce

Preheat oven to 350°F. Arrange six ¾-cup custard cups or ramekins in 13x9x2-inch baking pan. Combine cream, sugar, 2 tablespoons Marsala, and lemon peel in heavy medium saucepan. Stir over medium heat just until sugar dissolves (cream will be only lukewarm). Remove from heat. Whisk eggs and yolks in medium bowl until well blended. Whisk in cream mixture, then vanilla. Pour custard into cups, dividing equally. Pour enough hot water into baking pan to come halfway up sides of custard cups.

Bake flans until softly set in center, about 35 minutes. Remove flans from water bath and refrigerate uncovered until very cold and firm, at least 3 hours and up to 1 day.

Using knife, cut around flans in cups to loosen. Invert onto plates, shaking to dislodge if necessary. Stir caramel sauce in small saucepan over medium heat until warm, about 2 minutes. Whisk in remaining 3 tablespoons Marsala. Serve flans with caramel sauce.

6 SERVINGS

Chai Pots de Crème

CUSTARD

- 1 cup whipping cream
- 1 cup whole milk
- 1 tablespoon loose English Breakfast tea or Jasmine tea
- 1 cinnamon stick
- 8 whole cardamom pods
- 6 whole cloves
- 3 ¼-inch-thick rounds of peeled fresh ginger

- 4 large egg yolks
- ½ cup (packed) golden brown sugar
- ¼ teaspoon grated orange peel

TOPPING

- 1 cup chilled whipping cream
- 2 teaspoons sugar

FOR CUSTARD: Combine first 7 ingredients in medium saucepan. Bring to boil. Remove from heat; cover and let cream mixture steep 15 minutes to develop flavor.

Preheat oven to 325°F. Place six ¾-cup custard cups or ramekins in 13x9x2-inch metal baking pan. Pour cream mixture through fine strainer into medium bowl. Discard solids.

Whisk yolks, brown sugar, and orange peel in 4-cup measuring cup to blend well. Gradually whisk in cream mixture. Pour into custard cups, dividing equally (cups will not be full). Pour enough hot water into baking pan to come halfway up sides of custard cups. Cover baking pan with aluminum foil. Pierce foil in several places with skewer to allow steam to escape.

Bake custards until softly set (centers will move slightly when cups are shaken gently), about 30 minutes. Remove custards from water. Cool on rack. Chill until cold, about 4 hours. (*Can be made 1 day ahead. Cover; keep chilled.*)

FOR TOPPING: Beat whipping cream and sugar in medium bowl until soft peaks form. Place dollop of whipped cream atop each pot de crème and serve.

6 SERVINGS

Trio of Gelati

COFFEE GELATO

- 3 tablespoons dark rum
- 1½ tablespoons instant coffee granules
- ½ cup sugar
- 2 tablespoons cornstarch
- Large pinch of salt
- 2¼ cups whole milk

CHOCOLATE-ALMOND GELATO

- ½ cup slivered almonds (about 2 ounces), toasted, cooled
- ½ cup sugar
- 2 tablespoons cornstarch
- ⅛ teaspoon salt
- 2 cups whole milk
- 3 ounces bittersweet (not unsweetened) or semisweet chocolate, chopped
- ¼ teaspoon almond extract

ZABAGLIONE GELATO

- 1⅓ cups whole milk
- 4 large egg yolks
- ½ cup sugar
- ⅓ cup imported dry Marsala
- Large pinch of salt

FOR COFFEE GELATO: Mix rum and instant coffee in small bowl until coffee dissolves. Whisk sugar, cornstarch, and salt in heavy medium saucepan until no cornstarch lumps remain. Gradually whisk in milk. Cook over medium heat until mixture thickens and boils, stirring constantly, about 5 minutes. Remove from heat; whisk in coffee mixture. Press plastic wrap onto surface of gelato base. Refrigerate until cold, about 3 hours. Transfer gelato base to ice cream maker and process according to manufacturer's instructions. Transfer gelato to container; cover and freeze.

FOR CHOCOLATE-ALMOND GELATO: Combine almonds, sugar, cornstarch, and salt in processor; blend until nuts are finely ground. Transfer nut mixture to heavy medium saucepan. Gradually whisk in milk. Whisk over medium heat until mixture thickens and boils, about 5 minutes. Remove from heat. Add chocolate and whisk until melted. Mix in almond extract. Press plastic wrap onto surface of gelato base. Refrigerate until cold, about 3 hours. Transfer gelato base to ice cream maker and process according to manufacturer's instructions. Transfer gelato to container; cover and freeze.

FOR ZABAGLIONE GELATO: Combine ⅓ cup milk, egg yolks, sugar, Marsala, and salt in medium stainless steel bowl; whisk to blend. Place bowl over saucepan of simmering water

(do not allow bottom of bowl to touch water). Whisk until thick and thermometer registers 160°F, about 5 minutes. Remove bowl from over water. Whisk in remaining 1 cup milk. Press plastic wrap onto surface of gelato base. Chill until cold, about 3 hours. Transfer gelato base to ice cream maker and process according to manufacturer's instructions. Transfer gelato to container; cover and freeze. (*All gelati can be made 3 days ahead. Keep frozen.*)

8 SERVINGS

Lemon and Orange Sorbets in Citrus Cups

CITRUS CUPS

10 oranges

10 large lemons

ORANGE SORBET

1 cup sugar

3/4 cup water

1 tablespoon grated orange peel

2 cups fresh orange juice

LEMON SORBET

1 2/3 cups sugar

1 1/2 cups water

1 tablespoon grated lemon peel

1 cup fresh lemon juice

FOR CITRUS CUPS: Cut off top 1/3 of oranges and lemons; discard tops. Cut very thin slice of peel off bottoms to make flat. Scoop out fruit, leaving shells intact.

FOR ORANGE SORBET: Mix sugar, 3/4 cup water, and orange peel in heavy medium saucepan. Bring to boil, stirring to dissolve sugar. Remove from heat. Stir in orange juice; chill 1 hour. Process mixture in ice cream maker according to manufacturer's instructions. Spoon into orange shells, cover, and freeze at least 3 hours and up to 3 days.

FOR LEMON SORBET: Mix sugar, 1 1/2 cups water, and lemon peel in heavy medium saucepan. Bring to boil, stirring to dissolve sugar. Remove from heat. Stir in lemon juice; chill 1 hour. Process mixture in ice cream maker according to manufacturer's instructions. Spoon into lemon shells, cover, and freeze at least 3 hours and up to 3 days.

Place 1 orange cup and 1 lemon cup on each of 10 plates and serve.

10 SERVINGS

Baked Alaskas with Spiced Peaches and Raspberries

1 16-ounce frozen all-butter pound cake, thawed
1 quart or 2 pints peach ice cream

8 large egg whites
¼ teaspoon cream of tartar
1 cup powdered sugar

Spiced Peaches and Raspberries (see recipe on next page)

Cut cake on diagonal into eight ¹/₂-inch-thick slices. Using 3¹/₄-inch-diameter cookie cutter, cut out 1 round from slices; top with 1 scoop ice cream. Transfer to baking sheet. Freeze 1 hour.

Beat egg whites and cream of tartar in large bowl until soft peaks form. Gradually add sugar; beat until stiff peaks form, about 4 minutes. Transfer 1 cake-ice cream piece to work surface. Spread 1 scant cup meringue over, swirling to make peaks and covering completely. Return to sheet in freezer. Repeat with remaining cake-ice cream pieces and meringue. Freeze until firm, about 3 hours. (*Can be made 1 day ahead. Keep frozen.*)

Preheat oven to 450°F. Bake until meringue is light golden, about 5 minutes. Serve with Spiced Peaches and Raspberries.

8 SERVINGS

Spiced Peaches and Raspberries

1¾ pounds peaches, peeled, halved, pitted, sliced
1 tablespoon fresh lemon juice
¼ cup peach preserves, melted
¼ cup sugar
½ teaspoon ground cardamom
2 ½-pint baskets fresh raspberries

Toss peaches with lemon juice in medium bowl. Add preserves, sugar, and cardamom and toss. Let stand 10 minutes to allow flavors to blend. *(Can be made 4 hours ahead; cover and refrigerate.)* Add raspberries and toss gently.

8 SERVINGS

Coconut Milk Ice Cream with Ginger and Lime

1 4-ounce piece fresh ginger, peeled

2 13½- to 14-ounce cans chilled unsweetened coconut milk*
1 cup plus 2 tablespoons sugar
1 cup chilled half and half
5 tablespoons fresh lime juice
1 tablespoon grated lime peel
  Pinch of salt

2 mangoes, peeled, pitted, sliced
1 lime, thinly sliced

Finely grate ginger, then chop very finely. Set aside enough chopped ginger (including juices) to measure ⅓ cup.

Whisk coconut milk, sugar, half and half, lime juice, lime peel, salt, and reserved ⅓ cup grated ginger in medium bowl until sugar dissolves. Transfer mixture to ice cream maker. Process according to manufacturer's instructions. Transfer ice cream to container; cover and freeze until firm, about 3 hours. *(Can be prepared 3 days ahead.)*

Scoop ice cream into 6 stemmed glasses or bowls. Garnish with mango and lime.

*Available at Indian, Southeast Asian, and Latin American markets and many supermarkets.

6 SERVINGS

Royal Blueberry Ice Pops

2 ½-pint baskets fresh blueberries, rinsed, drained
1 8-ounce container blueberry yogurt
¼ cup water
¼ cup honey
2 tablespoons sugar

Combine all ingredients in processor and puree until smooth. Divide mixture among 8 ice pop molds (each about ¼ to ⅓ cup capacity). Cover and freeze until firm, at least 4 hours and up to 5 days.

MAKES 8

Lemon-Buttermilk Ice Pops

¾ cup sugar
5 tablespoons fresh lemon juice
2 tablespoons grated lemon peel
   Pinch of salt
1⅔ cups buttermilk

Whisk sugar, lemon juice, lemon peel, and salt in 4-cup measuring cup until sugar dissolves. Whisk in buttermilk. Divide mixture among 8 ice pop molds (each about ¼ to ⅓ cup capacity). Cover and freeze until firm, at least 4 hours and up to 5 days.

MAKES 8

Watermelon-Lemonade Ice Pops

2 cups (packed) finely chopped seeded watermelon
¾ cup frozen lemonade concentrate (½ of 12-ounce can), thawed
3 tablespoons sugar
   Pinch of salt

Combine all ingredients in processor. Puree until very smooth. Divide mixture among 8 ice pop molds (each about ¼ to ⅓ cup capacity). Cover and freeze until firm, at least 4 hours and up to 5 days.

MAKES 8

Dulce de Leche Ice Cream Pie with Mocha Fudge Sauce

CRUST

- ⅓ cup chopped pecans
- 2 tablespoons sugar
- ⅔ cup vanilla wafer cookie crumbs (from about 32 cookies)
- ½ teaspoon ground cinnamon
- 2 tablespoons (¼ stick) unsalted butter, melted

SAUCE

- 2 tablespoons boiling water
- 1 tablespoon instant espresso powder or instant coffee powder
- 1 cup sugar
- 2 tablespoons unsweetened cocoa powder
- 1 cup whipping cream
- ¼ cup light corn syrup
- 2 ounces unsweetened chocolate, finely chopped
- 2 tablespoons (¼ stick) unsalted butter
- 1½ teaspoons vanilla extract

- 2 pints caramel ice cream (such as dulce de leche)

- ½ cup chilled whipping cream
- 1 tablespoon powdered sugar
- 2 tablespoons chopped pecans

FOR CRUST: Preheat oven to 350°F. Blend pecans and sugar in processor until pecans are finely ground. Add cookie crumbs and cinnamon and process to combine. Add melted butter and blend until moist clumps form. Press crust onto bottom and up sides of 9-inch glass pie dish. Bake until crust is lightly toasted, about 10 minutes. Cool crust completely.

FOR SAUCE: Stir 2 tablespoons boiling water and coffee powder in small bowl until powder is dissolved. Whisk sugar and cocoa in heavy medium saucepan. Whisk in 1 cup cream, corn syrup, and coffee mixture. Add chocolate and butter. Bring to boil over high heat, stirring constantly.

Reduce heat to medium and simmer until slightly thickened, stirring occasionally, about 4 minutes. Cool 30 minutes. Stir in 1 teaspoon vanilla extract.

Soften 1 pint ice cream at room temperature 15 minutes. Spread evenly over bottom of crust. Drizzle 3 tablespoons sauce over ice cream. Freeze until sauce sets, about 15 minutes.

Meanwhile, soften remaining 1 pint ice cream at room temperature 15 minutes. Spread evenly atop sauce. Drizzle with 3 tablespoons sauce. Freeze pie until frozen, at least 4 hours. (*Sauce and pie can be made 1 day ahead. Cover and refrigerate sauce. Keep pie frozen.*)

Rewarm sauce over low heat, stirring often. Whip $1/2$ cup cream, powdered sugar, and $1/2$ teaspoon vanilla in medium bowl until peaks form. Transfer to pastry bag fitted with star tip. Pipe rosettes of cream around top edge of pie. Sprinkle with chopped pecans. Cut pie into wedges and serve with sauce.

8 SERVINGS

Toasted Almond Parfait

1 cup sugar
6 large egg yolks
$1/4$ cup light corn syrup
3 tablespoons amaretto
$1/2$ cup plus 3 tablespoons finely chopped toasted almonds

2 cups chilled whipping cream
2 teaspoons vanilla extract
2 ounces bittersweet (not unsweetened) or semisweet chocolate, finely chopped

Using handheld electric mixer, beat sugar, egg yolks, corn syrup, and amaretto in large metal bowl to blend. Place bowl over saucepan of simmering water (do not allow bottom of bowl to touch water). Beat until candy thermometer registers 160°F and parfait base is thick and billowy, about 8 minutes. Remove bowl from over water. Continue to beat parfait base until cool, about 7 minutes. Fold in $1/2$ cup almonds.

Beat cream and vanilla in another large bowl until soft peaks form. Fold cream into cool parfait base in 3 additions. Transfer parfait to 13x9x2-inch glass baking dish. Cover and freeze until firm, at least 4 hours and up to 2 days. Scoop parfait into goblets. Sprinkle with chocolate and 3 tablespoons almonds.

12 SERVINGS

Sports Bars with Dried Fruit and Peanut Butter

Nonstick vegetable oil spray
3 cups puffed whole grain cereal (such as Kashi)
½ cup walnuts, chopped
¼ cup chopped pitted dates
¼ cup chopped dried tart cherries
¼ cup raisins
⅓ cup creamy peanut butter
¼ cup honey
¼ cup light corn syrup

Preheat oven to 350°F. Spray 9-inch square metal baking pan with nonstick spray. Mix cereal, walnuts, dates, cherries, and raisins in medium bowl. Combine peanut butter, honey, and corn syrup in heavy small saucepan. Bring to boil, whisking constantly until mixture bubbles vigorously and thickens slightly, about 1 minute. Pour peanut butter mixture over cereal mixture in bowl; stir to blend. Transfer mixture to prepared pan; press to compact. Bake until just golden around edges, about 10 minutes. Cool completely. Cut into 2½x1½-inch bars. *(Can be prepared 3 days ahead. Store in single layer between sheets of foil in airtight container at room temperature.)*

MAKES ABOUT 18 BARS

Chocolate Mint Cookies

1½ cups all purpose flour
¾ cup unsweetened cocoa powder (preferably Dutch-process)
¼ teaspoon salt
¾ cup (1½ sticks) unsalted butter, room temperature
¾ teaspoon peppermint extract
½ teaspoon vanilla extract
1 cup sugar
1 large egg

6 ounces bittersweet (not unsweetened) or semisweet chocolate, chopped

COOKIES

Whisk flour, cocoa powder, and salt in medium bowl to blend. Using electric mixer, beat butter in large bowl until smooth. Beat in peppermint extract and vanilla extract. Beat in sugar in 3 additions. Add egg and beat until blended. Add dry ingredients and beat just until blended (dough will be sticky).

Divide dough between 2 sheets of plastic wrap. Using plastic wrap as aid, form dough on each into 2-inch-diameter log. Wrap with plastic and refrigerate dough until well chilled, at least 2 hours. *(Dough can be prepared 1 day ahead. Keep refrigerated.)*

Position 1 rack in center and 1 rack in top third of oven; preheat to 350°F. Line 2 baking sheets with parchment paper. Unwrap cookie dough logs; roll briefly on work surface to form smooth round logs. Cut dough logs crosswise into ¼-inch-thick rounds. Place rounds on prepared baking sheets, spacing 1 inch apart. Bake cookies until tops and edges are dry to touch, about 15 minutes. Transfer baking sheets with cookies to racks; cool completely.

Stir chocolate in top of double boiler set over simmering water until melted and smooth. Remove from over water. Cool melted chocolate until slightly thickened but still pourable, about 10 minutes. Dip fork into melted chocolate, then wave fork back and forth over cookies, drizzling melted chocolate thickly over cookies in zigzag pattern. Refrigerate cookies on baking sheets until chocolate is set, about 10 minutes. *(Can be made 1 week ahead. Refrigerate in airtight container between sheets of parchment paper or waxed paper.)*

MAKES ABOUT 3½ DOZEN

Oatmeal Lace Cookies

  1 cup sugar
 ½ cup (1 stick) unsalted butter, room temperature
 ¼ cup all purpose flour
  1 tablespoon vanilla extract
 ¼ teaspoon salt
 1½ cups old-fashioned oats

Using electric mixer, beat sugar and butter until well blended. Beat in flour, vanilla extract, and salt. Stir in oats. Cover and refrigerate cookie dough 1 hour.

Preheat oven to 350°F. Line 2 baking sheets with parchment paper. Roll dough by tablespoonfuls between palms into balls. Place dough balls on baking sheets, spacing 3½ inches apart (cookies will spread during baking). Using bottom of drinking glass as aid, flatten cookies to 1½-inch rounds. Bake until cookies are golden, about 11 minutes. Let cookies remain on sheets 1 minute. Using spatula, transfer cookies to racks and cool. *(Can be made 3 days ahead. Store cookies between sheets of waxed paper in airtight container at room temperature.)*

MAKES ABOUT 24

Raisin-Nut Spice Cookies

Nonstick vegetable oil spray

1 cup powdered sugar
8 teaspoons (about) whole milk
1 cup whole almonds (about 5 ounces), toasted, cooled
½ cup walnut pieces (about 2 ounces), toasted, cooled
1¾ cups all purpose flour
¾ cup (1½ sticks) unsalted butter, cut into ½-inch pieces, room temperature
⅔ cup sugar
1 teaspoon finely grated lemon peel
1 teaspoon finely grated orange peel
1 teaspoon aniseed
¾ teaspoon salt
½ teaspoon ground cinnamon
¼ teaspoon ground cloves
¼ teaspoon baking soda
2 large egg yolks
1 cup golden raisins

Position rack in center of oven and preheat to 350°F. Spray 2 large baking sheets with non-stick vegetable oil spray.

Place powdered sugar in small bowl. Mix in enough milk by teaspoonfuls (about 5) to form thick, smooth glaze. Cover glaze; set aside. Combine nuts in processor. Using on/off turns, blend until most nuts are reduced to ¼-inch pieces (some will be very finely ground). Combine flour, butter, sugar, citrus peels, aniseed, salt, spices, and baking soda in large bowl. Using electric mixer, beat at low speed until fine meal forms. Add egg yolks and beat until clumps form. Add nuts and raisins. Beat until dough holds together, adding milk by teaspoonfuls (about 3) if dough is dry. Knead dough briefly to compact.

Roll out ⅓ of dough on lightly floured surface to ¼- to ⅓-inch-thick rectangle. Cut lengthwise into 2-inch-wide strips. Cut each strip on diagonal into 1½- to 2-inch diamonds. Transfer diamonds to baking sheet. Gather dough scraps and reserve. Repeat with remaining dough. Reroll scraps, cutting out more cookies, until all dough is used.

Bake cookies, 1 sheet at a time, until golden, about 17 minutes. Spoon generous ½ teaspoon glaze over each hot cookie and spread with back of spoon to coat. Let cookies stand on baking sheets until completely cool and glaze is set. (*Can be prepared 1 week ahead. Store airtight between sheets of waxed paper at room temperature.*)

MAKES ABOUT 30

Chocolate Chocolate-Chip Cookies with Mocha Cream Filling

FILLING

- ½ cup semisweet chocolate chips (about 3 ounces)
- ½ cup whipping cream
- 1 tablespoon instant coffee granules
- ¾ cup powdered sugar
- 6 tablespoons (¾ stick) unsalted butter, room temperature
- 1 teaspoon vanilla extract

COOKIES

- 1 cup all purpose flour
- 3 tablespoons unsweetened cocoa powder
- 1 teaspoon baking soda
- ½ teaspoon salt
- ½ cup (1 stick) unsalted butter, room temperature
- ⅔ cup (packed) golden brown sugar
- ¼ cup sugar
- 1 large egg
- 2 teaspoons water
- 1 teaspoon vanilla extract
- 1 teaspoon instant coffee granules
- 2 cups semisweet chocolate chips (about 12 ounces)
- 1 cup pecans, coarsely chopped

FOR FILLING: Stir first 3 ingredients in heavy saucepan over medium heat until chocolate melts. Cool to room temperature, about 20 minutes. Using electric mixer, beat sugar, butter, and vanilla in bowl until blended. Beat in chocolate mixture. Refrigerate until beginning to firm, about 8 minutes. (*Can be made 2 days ahead. Cover and keep refrigerated. To use, let stand at room temperature until just soft enough to spread, about 2 hours.*)

FOR COOKIES: Preheat oven to 325°F. Line 2 baking sheets with parchment paper. Sift flour, cocoa, baking soda, and salt into bowl. Using electric mixer, beat butter and both sugars in bowl until well blended. Add egg, 2 teaspoons water, vanilla, and instant coffee; blend well. Beat in flour mixture. Stir in chocolate chips and pecans. Drop dough by tablespoonfuls onto prepared sheets, spacing 2 inches apart. Bake until tops are just firm to touch and no longer shiny, about 13 minutes. Cool cookies on sheets 10 minutes. Transfer to racks; cool.

Place half of cookies, flat side up, on work surface. Spread each with 1 tablespoon filling, leaving ¼-inch border. Top each with second cookie, pressing to adhere. Arrange on platter; cover and refrigerate at least 2 hours. (*Can be made 2 days ahead. Keep refrigerated.*) Serve cookies cold.

MAKES 20 SANDWICH COOKIES

Raspberry-Pecan Blondies

- 2 cups all purpose flour
- 1 teaspoon baking powder
- ½ teaspoon salt
- ¼ teaspoon baking soda
- 2 cups (packed) golden brown sugar
- ¾ cup (1½ sticks) unsalted butter, room temperature
- 2 large eggs
- 2 teaspoons vanilla extract
- 1 cup coarsely chopped pecans (about 3 ounces)
- 1 ½-pint basket fresh raspberries

Preheat oven to 350°F. Line 9x9x2-inch metal baking pan with aluminum foil, extending foil over sides by 2 inches. Butter and flour foil. Whisk 2 cups flour, baking powder, salt, and baking soda in medium bowl to blend. Using electric mixer, beat brown sugar and butter in large bowl until light and fluffy. Beat in eggs 1 at a time, then vanilla. Add flour mixture and beat just until blended. Stir in chopped pecans. Spread batter evenly in prepared pan. Sprinkle raspberries over top.

Bake dessert until top is golden and tester inserted into center comes out clean, about 50 minutes. Cool completely in pan on rack. *(Can be made 1 day ahead. Cover with plastic wrap and refrigerate. Bring to room temperature before serving.)* Cut into 16 squares and serve.

MAKES 16

Index

Page numbers in *italics* indicate color photographs.

Acknowledgments

RECIPES

Bruce Aidells
Alexandra and Eliot Angle
Pascal Aussignac, Club Gascon, London, England
Mary Corpening Barber
Melanie Barnard
Patrice Bedrosian
Lena Cederham Birnbaum
Blind Faith Café, Evanston, Illinois
The Blossom Deli, Charleston, West Virginia
BlueWater Cafe, New Canaan, Connecticut
Georgeanne Brennan
Cafe Matou, Chicago, Illinois
Carla Capalbo
Penelope Casas
Chez Betty, Park City, Utah
Circa 1886, Charleston, South Carolina
Jason Corrigan, A Touch of Garlic, Springfield, Massachusetts
Lane Crowther
Lori De Mori
Brooke Dojny
Sue and Mark Dooley
Dagny and Tim Du Val

Eccoqui, Bernardsville, New Jersey
Claudia Fleming
Janet Fletcher
Rozanne Gold
Ken Haedrich
Susan Haskell
Julie Hasson
Steve Hettleman
Thomas Houndalas
Michael Hunter
J. Benjamin's, Des Moines, Iowa
Michele Anna Jordan
Katharine Kagel
Jeanne Thiel Kelley
Elinor Klivans
Aglaia Kremezi
Lana Lazarus
Ledbetters', New Milford, Connecticut
Joyce Litz
Michael McLaughlin
Melvyn's, Palm Springs, California
Migis Lodge, South Casco, Maine
Mary Jo and Randy Miller
Kitty Morse
Old Mexico Grill, Santa Fe, New Mexico
David Page and Barbara Shinn, Home, New York

Barbara and Federigo Pardini, Pardini's Hermitage, Giglio, Italy
Patty and Luca Paschina
Yolanda Paterakis
Christine Piccin
Marion and Jean-Pierre Pinelli
Pinot Bistro, Studio City, California
Marcia Porch
Pam Proto and Rayme Rossello, Proto's Pizzeria Napoletana, Lafayette, Colorado
Victoria Abbott Riccardi
Eva and Georg Riedel
Rick Rodgers
Betty Rosbottom
Sally Sampson
Chris Schlesinger
Sarah Patterson Scott
Martha Rose Shulman
Marie Simmons
Susan Simon
Candida Sportiello
Joy and Alex Stewart
Suze, Dallas, Texas
Sandy Szwarc
Sarah Tenaglia
Diane and David Valcic
Aidita and Javier Vizoso
Hélène Wagner-Popoff

Joanne Weir
Sara Corpening Whiteford
Dede Wilson
Clifford A. Wright
Yarrow Bay Grill, Kirkland, Washington

PHOTOGRAPHY

Pascal Andre
Noel Barnhurst
Edmund Barr
David Bishop
John Blais
Wyatt Counts
Dasha Wright Ewing
Leo Gong
Jacqueline Hopkins
Brian Leatart
Ericka McConnell
Susan Gentry McWhinney
Pornchai Mittongtare
Raymond Patrick
Scott Peterson
David Prince
France Ruffenach
Mark Thomas